THE
CONCISE
GUIDE
TO
EXECUTIVE
ETIQUETTE

THE CONCISE GUIDE TO EXECUTIVE ETIQUETTE

■ ■ ■

Linda and Wayne Phillips

with Lynne Rogers

DOUBLEDAY

NEW YORK LONDON TORONTO SYDNEY AUCKLAND

PUBLISHED BY DOUBLEDAY
a division of
Bantam Doubleday Dell Publishing Group, Inc.
666 Fifth Avenue, New York, New York 10103

Doubleday and the portrayal of an anchor with a dolphin are trade-marks of Doubleday, a division of Bantam Doubleday Dell Publishing Group, Inc.

Library of Congress Cataloging-in-Publication Data

Phillips, Linda.
    The concise guide to executive etiquette / Linda and Wayne
Phillips, with Lynne Rogers.—1st. ed.
      p. cm.
    Includes index.
    1. Business etiquette. I. Phillips, Wayne, 1939–
II. Rogers, Lynne. III. Title.
HF5389.P55 1990
395'.52—dc20   89-32499
                                                  CIP

ISBN 0-385-24766-4 (pbk.)

This book is dedicated to Mary Miranda,
whose lifestyle truly epitomizes
the essence of the phrase
". . . consideration for others."

—L.M.P.
 W.R.P.

CONTENTS

THE
CONCISE
GUIDE
TO
EXECUTIVE
ETIQUETTE

CHAPTER ONE

THE IMPORTANCE OF IMPECCABLE BEHAVIOR

There is no accomplishment so easy to acquire as politeness, and none more profitable.
—George Bernard Shaw

A CHIEF EXECUTIVE OFFICER, SEEKING TO fill a highly visible position in his company, had narrowed the field to two equally desirable applicants. In a quandary as to which executive to choose, he took each out to dinner. The successful candidate? The one who ate the artichoke with aplomb.

Millions of today's executives know everything about their business except how to comport themselves in the business world. Education in the niceties of etiquette has not been part of their curriculum.

An investment banker who has mastered the intricacies of corporate mergers may have an abrasive manner that impedes her career progress.

A sales manager able to describe the gargantuan capabilities of his company's mainframe computer, or the sophisticated coverage offered by his firm's insurance policies, may find that extensive product fluency is not enough to make the sale in today's highly competitive market.

The ability to entertain a client with confidence, knowledge of how to use a business card without appearing overzealous or juvenile, ease at handling introductions with proper deference to the right people— those are some of the additional skills today's executive must have in order to work effectively with colleagues and clients.

We have designed this guide for the busy professional who wants to know simple rules of manners and behavior and who has neither the time nor the inclination to pore over traditional etiquette encyclopedias.

WHERE MANNERS
(AND RUDENESS) BEGIN

Until recently, children learned the rules of etiquette in the same way they learned language—by imitating their parents. Manners were not so much taught as they were absorbed. Sitting round the dinner table and watching the rest of the family day after day, year after year, youngsters could figure out when to pick up a spoon and how to hold it, when and how to use a fork, and how to manipulate it with a knife in order to cut their own portions into bite-size pieces. It certainly seemed as though knowing about table manners was something everybody was born with. Weren't they a matter of commonsense, after all?

The family table had been the center of social and political life since ancient times. In the oldest existing guide to general behavior, *The Instructions of Ptahhotep*, we learn that attitudes, values, and manners were expected to be passed from parent to child, handed down through successive generations, like rows added to an endless tapestry. That book, which was written on Egyptian papyrus about 2000 B.C. (and is still preserved in the Bibliothèque Nationale in Paris), was derived from an earlier work estimated to have originated circa 2500 B.C.—predating the assembling of the Bible by many centuries!

Recent decades have seen the unraveling of that age-old tradition. The typical American family now gets together about once a week, not around the dining table but in the multipurpose family room, where everybody can relax and watch TV while they eat. In a high percentage of homes, dinner is a prepackaged, precooked meal zapped to readiness within minutes in the microwave.

Should we expect a generation raised on fast food, finger food, and take-out food to know about forks, let alone which one to use?

Today's families may be typical only in their diversity. The majority of households are headed, not by mothers and fathers living together, but by single parents, most of whom work at full-time jobs. Grandparents, who for so long have been our symbols of continuity and guardians of traditional values, are no longer part of the household—they've moved away to communities for senior citizens. Increasingly, young people have been left to themselves.

Accustomed to roaming around in their private vehicles by age sixteen, listening to private sounds emanating from their stereo headphones, they could hardly be expected to develop an awareness of the rights of others, or an understanding of respect for one's elders.

Added to this social upheaval is the economic expansion of the past decades. Emerging industries have dramatically intensified the demand for skilled personnel—smart young people to carry on the world's business. To fill this need, a new population has come rushing into the marketplace, effectively eliminating some of the traditional barriers to employment. Positions which had previously been open only to white males of the "right" parentage are being filled by women and men whose backgrounds frequently do not include attendance at schools where etiquette was anyone's concern.

The lack of social skills evident among today's "new hires" has forced us to realize that, contrary to popular belief, good manners are not inherited, nor are they obvious to any intelligent person. Etiquette must be taught. In the interest of their own career advancement, executives need to master basic business and social protocol.

ON THE NEED FOR RULES

Without traffic signals driving would be chaos.

Think of it: as each vehicle approached an intersection, every driver would have to slow down almost to a halt to make certain there was no danger of hitting a pedestrian or being hit by a car coming from another direction. On sunny days, cars might weave from side to side along the road, as happy riders noticed lovely flowers, attractive mansions, strolling neighbors, or whatever.

Traffic regulations are the common language, the etiquette, of driving. The whole world knows that green is for go and red means stop. Yes, in some countries cars keep to the left side of the road, rather than the right—those are local customs, the manners of the specific area, which we take pains to learn about when we visit those places.

Traffic regulations make it possible for us to function in a world with automobiles.

The principles of social and business etiquette serve the same function as traffic signs: they provide us with a common language of behavior, so that people may meet, talk, dine, drink, travel, and do business with ease.

Manners are universally based upon the concept of consideration for others. While every society has its local conventions, it's not necessary to learn an entire litany of tribal rules every time you visit strangers. When people say, "Hello, come in, sit down, would you like to have a drink," we know that they are being courteous, and showing consideration for guests.

In business, this language of courtesy is of major importance, because the individual serves as the representative of a larger entity—the corporation. In the interest of the corporate balance sheet, companies need to know that their executives are putting forth the proper image.

Corporations whose representatives appear to be competent, confident, and considerate of others will be successful. They will enjoy a fine reputation and attract customers. As a result, good people will want to work there: morale, productivity, and profits will be high. This, in turn, will attract more business, and so the cycle continues.

Management understands that good manners make good sense.

Artificiality of Etiquette

All rules are artificial. As sociologists have often told us, civilization is artificial. However, society cannot exist without rules.

When people seek to dismiss etiquette as snooty behavior, they are referring to *bad* manners. Those who make others feel inferior or left out of the crowd are demonstrating a *lack* of courtesy.

Such rudeness is not a modern phenomenon. At the turn of the century, *Decorum*, a book of American etiquette, advised: "If you are with people who know less than you, do not lead the conversation where they cannot follow."

Appearance and Etiquette

The need to wear business clothes strikes young people accustomed to wearing designer jeans and sneakers as an attempt to stifle their personalities.

Personality is not what clothing is meant to show. Clothes may reveal taste, quality of workmanship, or the wearer's figure. Here again, it is the bad examples— poorly chosen, ill-fitting clothes—that call attention to themselves and make us uneasy.

Proper attire directs attention away from appearance and toward the content of the occasion; the meeting becomes the message. That's when personality—intelligence, charm, wit, and ability—can shine.

Business clothes can be considered a uniform: they are the costumes worn by people playing a part in the business world.

ORIGINS OF PROPER ETIQUETTE

The word *etiquette* comes from the French *étiquette* and literally means "ticket." The rules and regulations of the court were written on tickets, which were posted in the castle courtyard for all the lords and ladies to observe and obey.

Courtesy derives from *court behavior*. And so does curtsy, the low bow made by women at court to show respect for royalty.

Civility is rooted in the Latin word for *city*. Civility was an indication that one had acquired polish, as opposed to the crudeness of country behavior.

The Latin word for *polish* is the root of *politeness*.

Knights of old rode horses. The French word for horse, *cheval* has led to *chivalry*.

Modern Rules from Age-Old Customs

The ancient Egyptians, who gave the world the first guides to general behavior, were also first to use finger bowls. Everybody, including royalty, ate with their hands until the sixteenth century. Knives, spoons, and last of all, forks, are comparatively modern inventions. In those times, an invitation to dinner meant that you traveled with your own servants and brought your own chair.

The custom of dressing for dinner has been handed down from the ancient Romans, who slipped into loose robes at the beginning of the most important meal of the day. In fact, the word *companion* comes from the Latin and literally means "with bread," or "sharer of bread."

Many people think that dish covers were used as they are today, to keep food hot. Actually, they were designed to protect royalty from being poisoned. Once the chef had prepared the dishes and a member of the court had tasted them, they were covered and locked to guard against tampering, until dinner was served.

The first treatise on table etiquette was written by a Milanese monk, Bonvicino da Riva, in 1290. One of his bits of advice was: "Do not cross your legs on the laid out table."

Erasmus of Rotterdam exerted the most profound influence upon the etiquette of our civilization when he wrote *De Civilitate Morum Puerilium* (*On Civility in Children*, c. 1530): ". . . at the table the goblet and clean knife belong on the right, the bread on the left. When dishes of meat are brought to the table it is not correct to turn the dish around so that the better piece is before one."

As late as the seventeenth century, slices of round flat bread served as plates. An authority of the time decreed: "Do not lick your fingers *or* wipe them on the bread."

In the eighteenth century, George Washington copied this rule into his schoolbook: "Neither spit forth the stones of any fruit pie upon a dish, nor cast anything under the table. And, neither lean not on the table nor find fault with what you eat."

During the nineteenth century, American etiquette advanced as society did. City folk frequently took their cues from European precedent while rural societies evolved their own customs. The first decades of the twentieth century saw more than sixty-five books of etiquette published in the United States.

World War I turned our attention to other matters. With the advent of Prohibition, Americans seemed unconcerned about what was *de rigueur*. Movies and motor cars, bobbed hair and the Charleston were changing the way everyone behaved.

Then, in 1922, just when our standards appeared to be crumbling, Francis W. Crowninshield, the editor of *Vanity Fair*, persuaded a novelist named Emily Post to write a book on correct social behavior. *Etiquette: The Blue Book of Social Usage* became a runaway success.

In a revised edition issued a few years later, Mrs. Post appeared to have changed many of her positions on what was or was not appropriate. She told an interviewer: "Radical changes have taken place. . . . The young girls of today do pretty much as they like, and if they insist on smoking what can the old-fashioned people do about it? . . . The modern generation . . . does what it wants."

Mrs. Post understood that rules of etiquette develop slowly, but when the reason or the need for the rule disappears, the custom is discarded. Etiquette, like language, is ever-changing.

However, some rules remain constant: to stand as a sign of respect for an older person has been mannerly behavior for more than four thousand years.

NECESSARY BUSINESS SKILLS

This concise guide will take you step by step, course by course, through the fundamental etiquette involved in successfully courting a client, whether it be at breakfast, lunch, or dinner. We'll even steer you through the infamous cocktail party, and the newly popular corporate tea.

The goal of this book is not to teach executives how to set a fine table (although that will be an additional benefit) but to offer instruction in how to manage a table that has already been set. It is difficult, if not impossible, to project an image of poise and competence if one is waffling over the wine selection or sneaking glances at companions' hands in search of a clue to the proper use of the silverware.

As you will discover, etiquette is less a matter of arbitrary rules than a set of guidelines designed to help us maneuver through business situations without injuring another person's feelings or totaling our own ego with embarrassment. When everyone understands the rules, any occasion can be handled with genuine ease.

An executive can always be strong. But there is never any necessity to be mean. Consideration for others—courteous respect—is the keynote of etiquette. People are not considerate by nature; they learn to be. They realize that practicing the Golden Rule means when one behaves nicely to others those others will be nice in return.

This is not a book on business ethics but one of information that we hope enables you to better face the competitive world of business.

CHAPTER TWO

NEGOTIATING THE BUSINESS LUNCH

The world was my oyster,
but I used the wrong fork.
—OSCAR WILDE

AS A BUSINESSPERSON YOU'RE DOUBT-less aware that most business is conducted not at the conference table but in social situations. Your client wants to see that you are considerate, respectful, and capable.

Let's face it: people do business with people. And we like to do business with people we can trust.

The business lunch (or "power breakfast" or the newly fashionable afternoon tea) is your chance to communicate with the client on a one-to-one basis and will allow you to give a positive impression of the way you relate to strangers, instruct subordinates, and handle your utensils, as well as what your taste in food and drink is, and what you choose to talk about.

If you're quaking at the thought of passing such a formidable test, have no fear. All you need to do is practice a few simple skills.

This chapter will give you all the information you need to successfully navigate the business lunch.

PREDINING ETIQUETTE

The Invitation

Let's assume you are going to host a business lunch (or breakfast or tea) and it is you who must extend the invitation.

You should call the client expressly for this purpose.

If the client has called you about the project at hand, you have the opportunity to say, "Wouldn't it be a good idea if we got together to talk about this? How about having lunch?"

The client agrees, and you then set the date. Give the client a choice. For example: "Is next Wednesday convenient for you, or would Friday be better?"

CAVEAT: Don't set the date too far in advance. You risk losing the positive emotional chemistry that's operating at the moment you're making the appointment. Three weeks from the time of your phone call both of you may have forgotten exactly what you were talking about. If you and the client cannot get together for lunch within the next ten days it may be advisable to try to meet for breakfast or tea. (See Chapter 3, sections on "Power" Breakfasts and The Afternoon Tea.)

Next, focus on the place. It's a good idea to suggest two restaurants and let the client choose between them: "Would you like to go to The Bistro or the Steak House?"

When the client names the preferred restaurant, you then say, "Fine, I'll make the reservation. Shall we say twelve-thirty or one?" Again, you give the client the choice. Nowadays, there's another question to ask, "Smoking or nonsmoking?"

You then call the restaurant, make the reservation in your name, state the number of people in your party and the time you intend to arrive.

In your file of useful information, you should have a current list of places offering good service, pleasant atmosphere, food of good quality at moderate prices, and a variety of cuisines. Then, when you discover that the client likes Mexican, or French, or Southern, or some exotic type of cooking, you can come up with an appropriate recommendation.

If you're new in town and haven't yet discovered the smart dining spots, your colleagues or your superior can probably give you the names of a dozen reliable places right in the neighborhood.

You just want a comfortable place where you can be at ease. For you to choose the glossiest crystal-and-silver palace is pretentious, and draws attention to the place rather than to you. Save the glamour for when you and the client have something to celebrate—such as the better-than-anticipated results of your work.

The restaurant should be convenient, no more than a

few minutes from either of your offices. This is not the time to try "the little gem" that may be a gourmet's paradise but also happens to be forty minutes outside of town.

■ ■ ■

Lunch is a relatively recent phenomenon. It served to fill the huge gap between an earlier breakfast and a later dinner hour. It became fashionable during the latter part of the eighteenth century when it became the custom not to eat dinner until eight or nine o'clock.

The word lunch derives from lump, a piece of food. Ultimately, lunch became a very large meal which, in the Victorian era, divided the workday into two time periods—from nine to one and then two to six.

■ ■ ■

Clear Your Calendar

You've extended the invitation; set the date, place, and time; and made the reservation.

On your calendar, block out the time you will need. Be generous. Never risk interrupting the client with, "Ooops! I didn't realize how long we've been sitting here. I've got to run back to the office for an important meeting!"

Your client will know it's not his or her business you're attending to, and the warm, trusting relationship you've tried to establish will evaporate in less time than it takes for you to call for the check.

A Rehearsal of Sorts

If you've never dined at the restaurant, stop in a day before the scheduled appointment and introduce yourself to the host or maître d'. If your colleagues have recommended the place, the host or hostess will be glad to meet a new member of the team. If you're the first person from your office to patronize the establishment, he or she will want to make certain that everything goes well. In either case, you'll assure yourself of his or her attention.

Inspect the premises. Is the room large, possibly noisy? Is there a quiet alcove? If you see a particularly desirable table, reserve it. This is your performance, and you want everything working in your favor. Don't choose a table near the kitchen, the rest rooms, or the telephones.

Familiarize yourself with the menu, including the chef's specialties. If you have the time (and you can afford it), sample the food.

The more information you have, the more relaxed you'll be when you're there with the client.

The Day of Your Meeting

In the morning, reconfirm the time and place with the client or his or her secretary. Do this yourself rather than having your secretary make the call. (A breakfast meeting should be reconfirmed the previous afternoon.) Reconfirm with the restaurant as well.

When There's a Change of Plan

If, for some reason, your client asks to reschedule your appointment, *be certain to call the restaurant and cancel your reservation*. Failure to do so is rude, inconsiderate, and not only may rob someone else of the opportunity to dine at the restaurant but marks you as a no-show. A rash of no-shows can result in a half-empty restaurant because the owner, who thought he had a full house, turned away other calls for tables. No-shows are quite rightly despised by restaurateurs, who consistently list diners who don't honor reservations as their number-one problem. Imagine how you would feel if clients simply failed to arrive for their appointments with you.

Continued failure to obey this basic rule of restaurant etiquette may earn you the reputation of habitual no-show, which may affect the location of tables reserved for you and the cordiality—or lack of it—accorded you and your guests.

A reservation is your appointment with a place of business. Keep it, or call to reschedule.

AT THE RESTAURANT

Plan to arrive at the restaurant *at least ten minutes early*. This allows you time to check your coat and be ready to greet your client when he or she arrives. It is proper to wait at the door for your guest. However, if you are expecting more than one person, after the arrival of your first guest, wait only an additional ten minutes and then ask to be seated at your table, telling the maître d' that you are anticipating the arrival of another guest(s).

Seating Arrangement

Always offer the client the preferred seat. It's usually the one first pulled from the table. If a seat is not pulled out, you must quickly decide which is the preferred seat (the one with the best view, or the one that's most comfortable) and—even when a female host entertains a male client—give this place to your client.

Assign places to the other members of your party and see that your guests are seated before you sit down.

When you are seated, pick up the napkin, which should be to the left of your place setting, and place it unfolded (half-open if it is a large dinner size) across your lap. Don't tuck it into your shirt, your belt, or under your chin.

If, while dining, you must leave the table for any reason, just place the napkin loosely to the left of your plate. Don't refold it, and don't place it on your chair. The napkin stays in your lap until you are ready to leave the restaurant.

■ ■ ■

Napkins and forks have come and gone in our history. The Anglo-Saxons used forks as early as A.D. 800. Then for reasons that are not clear, the fork lost popularity and disappeared for about four hundred to six hundred years. During those centuries when forks were unknown, man used his hands to carry his food from the plate to his mouth. Everyone used napkins as large as today's towels to wipe the grease off their hands as they ate.

Once forks came back into general use—King Charles I used one in 1633, and suddenly they were fashionable again—the huge napkin was no longer necessary.

The smaller, less conspicuous napkin in use today covers the diner's lap and protects his or her clothes.

■ ■ ■

Ordering Drinks

The captain, waiter, or waitress will ask if you wish to order anything from the bar. Ask your client, "Would you care for a drink?"

If the client declines, so should you. "No, thank you," is all you need to say.

If the client orders a drink, good manners dictate that you have one, too. If your client orders an alcoholic beverage and you prefer not to drink alcohol, it's proper to order something such as club soda, a Bloody Mary without vodka, or fruit juice. You want the client to feel comfortable, so you do not let him or her drink alone.

When to Order the Meal

If the client wants a second drink, signal the waiter to serve another round. However, the good host as well as the smart businessperson, sees to it that everyone remains able to conduct the business of the meeting. When the second drink is served, ask for the menu, and focus on ordering the meal.

Mention the dishes the restaurant is noted for, recommend your personal favorites if you've dined at the restaurant before this, inquire about the chef's specials, and encourage your guest to order an appetizer as well as an entrée.

This is a way of letting your guest know that he or she need not confine himself or herself to ordering moderately priced entrées. You might even add, "The steaks are excellent here," or "I've enjoyed the lobster Newburg."

The guest's order is taken first. If there are others in the party, their orders are taken. You, as the host, order last.

If the client orders a first course—an appetizer, soup, or salad—you should do the same. You may ask the waiter to serve your salad when your guest's soup is served. Do the same with each course. In that way you are always dining together. Everyone is uncomfortable if one person eats while the other stares at an empty plate, waiting for the next course to be served.

Even if you are dieting, select a low-calorie dish for each course that your client orders. Eat only a small amount, if necessary. You may explain that you are watching your food consumption, but urge the others to enjoy themselves by saying, "The food is wonderful here, please enjoy!"

If You Are the Guest

Your host may give you no clues as to what to order, in which case you should confine yourself to the items in the mid-price range. You might ask your host, "What are you going to have?" or "What's really good here?"

CAVEAT: As guest or host, don't spend a great deal of time scrutinizing the menu. After all, you're at a business meeting, not a gastronomic event. If you fret about making such a minor decision you may cause others to wonder about your ability to act decisively in a business situation.

Proper Conversation

Unless the client brings up the subject, business is not discussed until after the meal has been ordered. Cocktail time is for getting-to-know-you conversation about important current events, business events, sports, hobbies, cultural matters, your other interests, the client's, friends you may have in common, amusing anecdotes.

Politics, finances, and religion are unsuitable topics, as is gossip about people in either company.

What About Smoking?

If the client has requested that your table be in the non-smoking section of the restaurant, obviously you should not smoke.

Even if you happen to be dining in one of the few places that does not have smoking and nonsmoking sections, unless the client lights a cigarette, you should not smoke.

It's that simple. You shouldn't even ask permission. Failure to observe this rule could cost you the account!

Of course, if the client has requested the smoking section, and lights a cigarette (cigars or pipes are unacceptable in a restaurant), you may smoke also, but only after coffee has been served. You don't smoke during the meal.

Taking Command of the Situation

Once you have ordered your meal, you are free to bring up the subject of business—the reason for your lunchtime meeting.

Ideally, you should have only one or two items on your main agenda, not a laundry list of topics. Your goal is to establish an easy, considerate, trusting relationship with your client; to do that, you need to be able to listen attentively, ask questions, discuss your differences fully, and reinforce your areas of agreement. Racing from one topic to another is counterproductive, imposes pressure, and tends to make you look like someone who's trying to run the whole show. That's not the impression you wish to give.

It's quite possible that you won't know the answer to a question your client will ask. Be honest. A simple, "I don't have that information, but I'll get it for you by tomorrow afternoon," is a straightforward response your client can respect.

While conducting your business dialogue, you also need to pay attention to the service. As host, it's up to you to see that everyone at your table is served properly. You should be the one to signal the waiter and ask for a missing spoon, more bread and butter, the pepper mill, drinking water, or whatever is wanted. Ask your guests if everything is to their liking. If the steak is well done when your guest ordered it rare, if a hot dish is served barely warm, if there are bones in the fish fillet, call the maître d', who will have the dishes removed and replaced.

CAVEAT: When the food or the service are unsatisfactory, don't complain aloud to your guests. Speak to the owner or the manager after you have said good-bye to your guests.

Bringing the Meal to a Close

After everyone at the table has finished the entrée and salad, the waiter or captain will return with the dessert menu or possibly wheel the dessert cart to the table to tempt you. Assuming that you have sufficient time, you, as host, should encourage your guest(s) to have dessert. If your guest orders dessert, you should select one as well.

If your guest only wants coffee you should forego dessert even though it may be your favorite part of the meal. Ask if he or she wishes regular or decaffeinated, then ask the waiter if the restaurant serves brewed decaffeinated coffee—thereby giving your guest this additional choice.

When your coffee is served, ask the waiter to bring your check.

Use this time to review what has been discussed—agreements arrived at, information still to be obtained. Make sure you and your guest understand what's supposed to happen next, who is responsible for what action.

If a follow-up meeting is necessary, set at least a tentative date for your next meeting.

Paying the Bill

Settle the bill quietly at the table with your credit card, adding in the tips for the waiter and captain. If you have a personal or company charge account, sign the bill.

If you are paying by check, or if you feel compelled to verify the accuracy of every item on the bill, don't do this at the table in front of your guest. And never, never whip out your pocket computer to check the waiter's addition or try to figure how much to tip! Instead, excuse yourself, go to the captain's station or the front desk, and settle the bill there.

Female Executives as Hosts

A male guest of a female executive may sometimes insist on picking up the check. The businesswoman may handle this easily by telling her client, "Please, you're the guest of ABC Corporation, and they are delighted to treat you to lunch!"

This response depersonalizes the situation; it's no longer a male-female transaction.

Whom to Tip and How Much

The custom of tipping dates from the mid-eighteenth century. The tip was originally a small gratuity placed on the table *before* the meal (presumably for the server to keep an eye on while serving) *To Insure Promptness* or, as some historians say, *To Insure Prompt Service*. When the meal was finished, the server, having been prompt and earned the gratuity, pocketed the tip.

In this country, where tipping is considered voluntary, the amount of a tip is left to individual discretion. Elsewhere in the world, a preset percentage is added to one's bill as a service charge.

Because tipping customs seem to vary even from one neighborhood to the next, Americans often allow the business of tipping to embarrass, frighten, or just plain bewilder them. Under normal circumstances, here's how to tip when you're at a restaurant:

The maître d' receives five or ten dollars (depending upon the elegance of the restaurant) in cash, in a handshake either at the start of your meal or as you leave the restaurant. You say "Thank you" as you shake his (or her) hand.

The captain (or whoever takes your order) receives 5 percent of the check, either in cash, in a handshake, or specified on your bill.

The waiter receives 15 percent of the check, specified on the bill. (In areas such as New York City, where the tax on restaurant dining is 8¼ percent, most people simply double the tax.)

The head waiter gets 5 percent. If you've also been served by him.

The sommelier (wine steward) expects 10 to 15 percent of your wine bill. You may give this to him in a handshake. (For more on selecting and serving wines, see Chapter 3, Making Wine Selection Simple.)

To many people this seems like a cumbersome process when you're trying to breeze through your lunch with a certain amount of style. If you prefer, write a fairly generous amount—20 percent is ideal—on the *tip* line of your credit card voucher, and let the staff handle it themselves.

Yes, if service has been dreadful you *may* decide not to tip! You should also tell the manager what you're doing and why, so that he or she can try to remedy the situation.

If service has been superb, and you and your guest(s) have been treated like royalty, reward the excellent performance—and commend those people to management as well.

Carbon Copies

Along with your credit card, the waiter will hand you your customer's receipt with two pieces of carbon paper still attached to it. He's not being disrespectful (as one young lady with whom we recently dined mistakenly assumed). The restaurant is trying to protect you against the thieves who copy credit card names and numbers from carelessly discarded carbons and then proceed to steal millions of dollars worth of merchandise by charging it to other people's accounts.

Until all the credit card companies design a foolproof, carbonless receipt, it is essential that you tear up the carbons so that no one has access to your account number.

If you don't care to soil your fingers or leave a mess on the table, why not fold the carbons and place them, with the receipt, in your wallet, pocket, purse, or briefcase, to dispose of when you return to your office.

Who Thanks Whom, and How

You, as host, escort your guest to the door—taking care of your coats if you've checked them—shake hands, and thank your guest for taking the time to join you for such a productive meeting. Remind the client when you expect to see one another again or, if no date has been set, promise to call to set an appointment time before the end of the week.

The guest thanks the host, praises the choice of restaurant (unless the food and service have really been dreadful) and, within the next two days, sends a handwritten thank-you note. An executive whose scrawl is illegible may send a typewritten thank you.

The Guest Who Won't Say Good-bye

There may be times when a client is such an enthusiastic conversationalist, is so delighted with the restaurant and with you, that your luncheon lasts far longer than anyone could have anticipated. If this extended meeting threatens to impinge on your relationship with another client, you'll have to decide which meeting is more important to you and to your company. If it makes more sense for you to stay where you are, excuse yourself from the table, call your office, and try to reschedule any appointments you will not be able to keep.

What if you absolutely must leave to attend a more important meeting? Is there a way to get out of this gracefully?

Catherine W. is an account executive for a very large catering corporation. Her lunch with Mr. Sloane had gone well: he had given her the order for his company's annual banquet. While he wanted to discuss the menu and decor, he seemed to be growing more loquacious with each sip of his brandy. She feared that he had no need—or intention—to return to his office and might want to continue talking until it was time for him to go straight home. Another client was due to arrive at Catherine's office within minutes. Finally, she said to her luncheon guest, "Mr. Sloane, I understand how important these details are for the success of your program. And I really wish we could make these decisions right now. But as it happens, my associate is away on business and I'm covering for him. He has an appointment in ten minutes which I am going to have to handle for him. Would you be good enough to excuse me? I'll call you tomorrow and go over the entire program with you so that we can be sure everything is exactly as you want it to be."

This is a solution that recognizes a client's importance and yet suggests that there are unavoidable demands on one's time which in no way supersede the client's, but nevertheless must be met.

Catherine might also have telephoned her office and made arrangements for someone equal in rank to meet her other client, explain that her meeting was lasting longer than expected, and act as her substitute.

It's also possible to instruct your secretary to phone you at the restaurant if you have not returned by a certain time. This may be a bit theatrical but permits you to explain to your guest that circumstances beyond your control prevent you from continuing your lunch together.

CHAPTER THREE

DINING ETIQUETTE

Ever since Eve ate apples
much depends on dinner.
—Byron

To BE TOTALLY COMFORTABLE IN THE role of host/executive you must be able to focus on your client, not on which knife or fork to use.

It may seem a bit of a paradox—learning how to eat, so that you never need to think about it.

How can you attain that dining ease?

The same way you become proficient at tennis, skiing, playing the guitar, driving a car, or running a computer: practice.

Practice, practice, practice.

THE TABLE SETTING

The place setting we show illustrates the most formal setting you'll ever encounter. It's for a style of dining service called *à la Russe*—Russian style—in which an already filled plate is never set in front of a diner; instead, the courses are individually served at the table by a waiter, one for each diner. If you can master the *à la Russe* service, you can manage any table setting.

The Map of the Table

There are three forks to the left of the service plate; three knives to the right. You should never find more than three of one utensil at a place setting.

The only exception will be the fourth fork, the small oyster fork, which is placed at the extreme right of the place setting. The tines should be resting in the bowl of the soup spoon.

The fork resting in the bowl of the soup spoon is used for oysters or shrimp cocktail. After the soup spoon, and working from outside to inside on both sides, are the fish fork and fish knife, followed by the meat fork and knife. Next to the dinner plate are the salad fork and knife. Glasses shown are: the sherry glass is positioned above the soup spoon (sherry being served to accompany soup); the white wine glass (for fish) is above the fish knife; and the red wine glass (served with meat) is located above the meat knife. Behind the red wine glass is the water goblet. The champagne flute (to accompany dessert) is adjacent to the water goblet.

There's a simple rule to remember about cutlery: always start from the outside and work your way, course by course, toward the center.

Now, let's proceed with dinner.

The First Course

The oyster fork is used to eat clams, oysters, and that most popular of appetizers, the shrimp cocktail. Because shrimp cocktail is frequently served in a pedestal dish, you never cut the shrimp with a knife—that might topple the pedestal—but rather eat it by taking several bites. (If shrimp is served on a flat plate, you may use your knife to cut.) The lettuce in the dish is for garnish only, not to be eaten.

The waiter (or waitress) will remove the shrimp cocktail dish from the right, leaving the service plate on the table. He will then place a soup dish and plate upon the service plate and proceed to serve the soup from the left.

The Soup Course

The next utensil on your right is *the soup spoon*. Grasp it at the end of the handle, with your thumb on the top. Lean forward slightly, so as not to spill any food in your lap, and dip the spoon sideways into the soup at the edge nearest you. Merely skim the surface of the liquid, moving the spoon away from you.

In this way, you avoid the possibility of splashing hot soup into your lap and at the same time you touch only the coolest surface of the liquid. Practice this motion until it becomes easy for you.

Sip from the side of the spoon, don't put the entire spoon in your mouth. And sip silently, without noisy slurps.

If you wish to get every last spoonful, lift the rim of the soup plate slightly to tip the bowl away from you, and continue to spoon the soup from the outer edge of the bowl.

When you're done, leave the spoon resting on your plate.

Sometimes soup is served in a cup with a handle—ears—on each side. It's perfectly appropriate to pick up the cup by both handles and sip the soup. When you've finished, place the spoon on the small plate underneath the cup.

A diner never tries to do two things at the same time: If you are served crackers with your soup course, put the soup spoon down and take a bite of the cracker. Don't hold the cracker in one hand, the soup spoon in the other, and alternate between them. You can resemble a reciprocating saw and the motion becomes distracting.

You don't break crackers into the soup. In the unlikely event that large crackers are served, break off a bite-size portion, as you would with bread (see below), keeping the unused part of the cracker on the under plate. If oyster crackers are served, place them on your under plate and add a few at a time to your soup.

Where's the Bread and Butter Plate?

There are no bread and butter plates at this table because rolls or bread and butter would not be served at a formal dinner. Nor should you ask for them.

However, at your business luncheon—as well as at dinner in the finest restaurants—you will find the small bread and butter plate at your left or what is sometimes called a sideplate. A separate utensil, the *butter knife*, may be resting on the plate. If there is none, it is appropriate to use your dinner knife to butter your bread or roll.

In very casual restaurants you may find only a bread basket on the table along with a communal butter dish. Offer the basket to your guests before serving yourself. Use your fork to put a pat of butter on your entrée plate and leave your bread or roll on the table.

Always break bread—never cut it—and then butter only a small piece that can be eaten in one bite. Do the same with rolls—breaking off only a small portion-size piece. It's inappropriate to sit at the table with half a buttered roll in your hand, taking bites of it between witty remarks.

The tradition of breaking bread is an ancient one, and is written about in the Talmud. By breaking off only the small amount that was actually going to be eaten, one did not contaminate the remainder of the bread, which then could be distributed to the poor.

The Fish Course

Your waiter will remove the service plate and replace it with a heated plate for the fish course. The *fish knife* has an unusual, swordlike shape that is easily recognizable. (See table setting illustration, page 28.) It was introduced in the nineteenth century—during Queen Victoria's time—to assist in deboning fish, which in those days was brought to the table whole, and served with head and tail still intact.

Hold the fish knife as you would a pencil, so that you can use the broad side of the blade delicately to lift and separate sections of the fish.

There's no reason to be intimidated by the fish knife! In fact, if you're served a boneless fillet, you don't even have to use it; leave it on the table and cut the fillet with the side of your *fish fork*—that's the fork on your extreme left, which resembles a salad fork except that the tines are wider. You may, however, use your knife as a "pusher" if you are eating in the Continental or European style (see below).

Serving Oneself

At a formal banquet, food is removed from the right (easy to remember because "remove" and "right" begin with R) and served at your left.

When the waiter presents the platter, take the serving fork in your left hand and the spoon in your right. Place a portion on your plate and set the serving pieces side by side on the platter.

The Main Course

The *entrée*, or *dinner knife* and *fork* are the larger utensils and will be used next when the main course, usually meat or poultry, is served.

American vs. European or Continental Style

Americans are fork-shifters. To cut their food they hold the fork, tines down, in their left hand, and with the knife in their right hand, they cut just one bite-size piece of food (never more than two, certainly). Then they rest the knife along the rim of the plate, *shift the empty fork to the right hand*, tines up, and use the fork to pick up that piece of food and carry it to their mouth.

Each time they wish to cut another morsel, they shift the fork back to the left hand, pick up the knife, cut the meat, put the knife down, shift the fork to the right hand, then pick up the meat and bring it to their mouth. Sounds like a lot of work, doesn't it?

In the European or Continental style, the fork remains in the left hand, tines down, throughout. The handle of the fork fits into the palm of the hand, and the forefinger is extended to the base of the handle, for greater leverage. As each piece of food is cut, it is brought to the mouth with the fork held in the left hand. The knife is held in the right hand and is also used as a food pusher.

Many people feel that the European method is more efficient and more sophisticated. Either method is appropriate. Whichever style you use, it is important to remember to sit up straight and bring the food up to your mouth; don't bend down to the table to bring your mouth to the food.

Once the knife has been used, it is placed diagonally along the edge of the plate—imagine the blade pointing to eleven o'clock, while the handle rests at two o'clock. It is never appropriate to lean your knife and fork sideways—half on the table and half on the plate—as if they were oars.

We are frequently asked why, when the Continental style seems so efficient, Americans changed their eating style. Many people wonder why the pragmatic Pilgrims would have developed such a cumbersome way of using knives and forks. They are always surprised to learn that it was the *Europeans* who changed, not the Americans.

When the use of knives and forks became popular in Europe at the start of the seventeenth century, everyone ate with knife and fork the way most Americans do today. However, the upper classes in European society noticed that the masses were eating with the same utensils as they and, wanting to differentiate themselves as members of the upper class, they began eating with the fork held in the left hand and the knife in the right.

The final result? All Europeans began eating in this same way.

CAVEAT: Whether you're eating in the American or the Continental style, it's never appropriate to pile food on the fork and then deposit it in your mouth. Nor should you spear a piece of bread or roll on the end of your fork and propel it all around the plate, mopping up the gravy or juice, no matter how delicious it may be. If you must have every last drop of liquid, take a bit of bread in your fingers and dip it into one spot on the plate. Continue in this way until you've satisfied your craving.

The Silent Service Code

At formal banquets, and at good restaurants, the staff should be able to tell merely by the positions of the knife and fork whether the diner has paused to carry on a conversation, wishes a second helping, or has finished eating.

Lively conversation is the ingredient that guarantees the success of any occasion. When you speak, your utensils should be in the *resting position*: fork crossed over the knife, tines down.

To indicate that you have *finished eating*, set your knife and fork, tines down, parallel to one another, diagonally across the plate. Imagine the handles at four o'clock and the tines at ten o'clock.

If you'd like a *second helping*: set the knife and fork, parallel, along the rim of the plate. The handles will be at two o'clock, the blade and tines near eleven o'clock.

As we say, at the best restaurants everyone should know the code. However, if your particular waiter or waitress doesn't seem to be familiar with the language of silent service, raise your hand quietly to get his (or her) attention and, once you've made eye contact, speak softly—almost mouthing the words—"waiter" or "waitress."

The terms: sir, miss, honey, ma'am, etcetera are all inappropriate forms of identifying the service people when attempting to get their attention.

Nor should you wave your hand frantically or raise your voice. If you have difficulty getting your waiter's attention, tell the captain to have the waiter come to your table.

Salt and Pepper

Although we invariably ask, "Will you please pass the salt?" the salt and pepper always travel together. Place both shakers on the table in front of the person requesting them.

Instead of the salt *shaker*, you may find a little dish of salt. This is the salt *cellar*. You pass the salt cellar with the pepper shaker.

The salt cellar usually has an accompanying tiny salt spoon. Use it to place a spoonful of salt at the edge of your plate and dip each forkful of food into that.

If there's no spoon, use the edge of your clean knife to serve yourself a portion of salt.

CAVEAT: Never salt your food before tasting it: that's insulting to the chef and, by extension, to the host. And never ask for ketchup, for the same reason.

The Salad

The American custom of serving salad as a first course is a recent innovation, dating approximately from the 1950s, that appears to have originated on the West Coast, where health-conscious Californians decided that chewing lettuce at the start of a meal was somehow beneficial. Until that time, salad was served *after* the entrée—in this country as it is in restaurants throughout the world.

There's a logical reason for this: the vinegar or lemon juice in salad dressing will adversely affect the taste of the wine served with the entrée.

At a formal banquet and in fine restaurants, the tradition is still observed.

The *salad fork* and *knife* are the small pair closest to the plate. Yes, it is appropriate to use your knife to cut a lettuce leaf to bite size.

When the salad is not set in front of you as a separate course, the salad plate will be on your left, above the bread and butter plate. You'll never be confused if you remember that plates are on your left, while glasses—or beverages—are on the right.

When entrée and salad are served at the same time, you may use the entrée fork for both.

After the salad your waiter will clear the table. The salt and pepper shakers are removed and crumbs are swept away.

Although the glasses are left on the table, this is the only time that there is no plate in front of you. It's as if the curtain were down for a brief intermission before the next scene, which in this case will be the dessert course.

Before we discuss dessert, let's examine the crystal.

Which Glass to Use

Glasses follow the same logical progression as the silverware, moving from right to left, from the outside toward the center.

Identify the glasses in the illustration (see page 28).

The Y-shaped glass positioned just above the soup spoon is the *sherry glass*. Sherry will frequently be served as an accompaniment to soup.

White wine is customarily served with fish, and the *white wine glass* will be above the fish knife.

For the meat course, there is the *red wine glass*. Notice that it's larger than the white wine glass.

Largest of the glasses is the *water goblet*. This glass will be nearest the center.

If champagne is to be served, you'll see the tall, slender champagne *flute* or the saucer-shaped caterer's glass. Champagne is frequently served with dessert.

Only the sherry glass is removed from the place setting—when the soup plates are cleared. All of the others—the water goblet, the red and white wine glasses—remain on the table, so that you may sip from them as you please throughout the course of the meal.

The Dessert Course

Your waiter will bring the dessert plate, upon which will be the finger bowl on its doily, flanked by the dessert fork and spoon.

Place the silver on either side of the plate. Put the bowl and doily on the table, to the upper left of your plate.

According to the European or Continental style, you eat with the spoon and use the fork as a pusher. Of course, if you're eating American style, you may use whichever utensil you prefer—and leave the other on the table.

At a very formal dinner, you may be served three desserts: ice, sweets, and, lastly, fresh fruit. A fresh plate is brought for the fruit, as well as another pair of utensils, the small *fruit knife* and *fork*.

Apples or pears are quartered with the fruit knife.

You may peel them if you wish. Then you cut them into bite-size pieces, which you eat either with the fruit fork or with your fingers. Grapes are always eaten with your fingers.

Finger Bowls

Dip the tips of your fingers into the finger bowl. Wipe them on the napkin in your lap. If you wish, you may touch the tips of your moistened fingers to your lips, and then lightly touch your napkin to your lips.

Dealing with Accidents

If you happen to drop your silverware on the floor, ignore it—unless it is a safety hazard to others. If so, merely use your foot to move it out of the flow of traffic. In any case, simply pick up the next utensil in line and continue.

If you accidentally topple your water goblet, set it right as quickly as possible.

Should you accidentally spill water on the person next to you, offer your napkin and apologize for the accident. It's not necessary to try to mop up the spill yourself.

Remember, the waiters and the rest of the staff are there to help, not intimidate you. It's their job to be alert and to know what to do, quickly and quietly.

Eating Special Foods

At our seminars on dining etiquette, people invariably ask how to deal with certain unusual or difficult foods. Our first bit of advice is: Be your own best friend, and try to select foods that are easy to manage with your knife and fork.

That may sound like sidestepping the issue, but as we've said before in this chapter, the restaurant is merely the setting for a business discussion; what you eat is incidental to what you expect to accomplish, and that is to establish a positive relationship with your client.

For those occasions when you don't have a choice, when the food is preselected and you've got to make the best of it, we offer some specific guidelines:

Apples and pears: At a formal dinner, when the fruit knife and fork are presented, quarter and peel the fruit (if you wish), then slice into bite-size pieces and eat with a fork.

Apricots: At a formal dinner, halve the apricot, cut out the pit, and eat with a fork.

Artichokes: May be served hot or cold. Tear off one leaf at a time, dip the broad end into the accompanying melted butter or Hollandaise sauce, then bring it to your mouth and gently draw the meat out by running the leaf between your teeth. Place the leaves neatly on your plate (if a separate bowl isn't provided). You will come to the fuzzy choke, which is inedible. Remove it with your knife and fork to reveal the saucer-shaped artichoke heart, which should be eaten with a knife and fork. Because you've used your fingers to eat the leaves, you should be served a finger bowl when you've finished.

This time-consuming ritual draws your attention away from the client, who should be your prime concern, and is not an appropriate choice for a business lunch. Our motto is: *avoid the artichoke*.

Asparagus: These *are* finger foods. It is okay to pick up a stalk at the base, dip the tip into the accompanying sauce, and bite off the head. Many people are unaware of this, however, so if your client uses knife and fork to cut asparagus, by all means do the same.

Individual tongs are sometime brought in with asparagus; they may be used instead of your fingers, to grasp the base.

When asparagus are overcooked and limp, it's best to use your knife and fork.

Any part of the base that's too tough to chew is left on the side of the plate.

Avocado: If it's served cut in half with the pit removed, eat it with a spoon.

Peeled, cut up, and served in a salad, it's eaten with a fork.

Bacon: The correct way to eat bacon is with a fork. If it's extremely crisp and dry, the fingers may be used.

Baked Potato: Cut an X in the top, squeeze the potato slightly with your fingers, then add butter and/or sour cream.

Bananas: In a formal setting, the banana should be peeled, cut into slices, and eaten with a fork.

Berries: In a formal setting, berries are eaten with a spoon. A large berry, such as a strawberry, may be eaten with a fruit fork and knife. If the berries are served whole with the hull attached, you may hold each at the hull and dip the berry into the accompanying sauce or cream.

To eat the currently popular giant chocolate-dipped strawberries, insert the fork into the flesh near the stem, then slice the berry vertically, very carefully, so as not to splinter the chocolate coating.

Butter: Use the dinner fork to bring the butter to your plate; use the butter knife to spread butter on bread. As we've noted, there's no bread and butter plate at a formal dinner.

Butter is put on a baked potato with your fork, not your knife.

Canapés: Served before a meal, they are finger foods; served at the table, they are eaten with a fork.

Cherries (or other fruit with pits): If they're eaten with the fingers at an informal setting, remove the pit by putting your hand to your mouth and placing the pit on the edge of your plate. At a formal setting, when served in a dessert such as cherries in ice cream, a spoon is used. Bring the spoon to your mouth and, unobtrusively, spit the pit into the spoon and place it on the edge of your plate.

Chicken: Unless you're at a picnic or barbecue, chicken is not a finger food! Always use your knife and fork.

Chops of any kind: The same rule holds true: we know that the tastiest meat is closest to the bone, but if you can't cut it off with your knife and fork, the meat must remain on your plate.

Clams: Whether they are baked or served on the half shell, clams are eaten in one bite. Use the oyster fork to pick up the clam. You may then pick up the shell and drink the remaining clam juice.

Steamed clams: Open the shell and with your fingers pull away the black outer skin covering the neck. Holding on to the neck, dip the clam into the accompanying broth or melted butter, and eat it in one mouthful. This complicated, time-consuming, and potentially messy ritual makes steamers inadvisable at a business lunch.

Corn on the cob: This is best reserved for family occasions. If the ear of corn is large, break it in half. Butter only a small portion at a time to avoid dripping. Hold it at the end in both hands and eat.

Eclairs: These are best eaten with a fork.

Eggs: To eat a boiled egg in a cup, crack the shell gently with a knife, lift off the shell, and place it on the edge of the plate. Steady the egg cup with one hand and eat the egg with the other hand, using a spoon.

Escargots (snails): Served with a special pair of tongs and a double-pronged fork. Grip the snail shell in the tongs, and pick out the snail with the fork. If there's bread at the table, it's perfectly correct—and delicious —to dip the bread into the garlic sauce after you've eaten the snails.

Fish (when served whole): Slit the fish from gill to tail, just above the middle of its side. Fold back the skin and, with knife and fork, remove bite-size portions of the meat. As you do this, the backbone of the fish will be revealed. Insert the knife under one end of the backbone, and gently lift it out with your fork. Set the bone on the side of the plate. Eat the remaining meat with a fork. Remove any bones from your mouth with your thumb and forefinger.

French fries: At noncasual settings, use your fork to cut the fries into bite-size pieces. If you're using ketchup, place a dollop on the side of the plate and dip the fries into it.

Grapefruit: Generally served cut in half, with the sections loosened. Eat with a spoon, preferably the grapefruit spoon, which has a pointed tip and serrated edge.

Lobster: Unless lobster is served out of the shell, as in a salad or as lobster Thermidor, this is another food that you should not order in a business situation. Your concentration goes to cracking the shell, extracting the meat, and trying not to squirt the juice on the person seated opposite you, your client! Save this glorious food for occasions when you can relax and enjoy it—such as informal dinners with friends or family.

Mussels: When they're served in the shell, you may use one of two methods: pick them up by the shell and spear the mussel with an oyster fork, or replace the fork with an empty mussel shell, using it as a scoop to extract each mussel from its shell.

Oysters (served on the half shell): Steady the shell on the plate with one hand, and with the other hand use an oyster fork to lift out the oyster, which you then plop into your mouth whole and chew, if necessary. You may pick up the shell and drink the juice after you've eaten the oyster.

Oysters in a stew are eaten with a spoon. Fried oysters are eaten with a knife and fork.

Parfait: Start at the top and, using the long, slender parfait spoon customarily served with this dessert, inch your way down to the syrup at the bottom. Don't try to stir the syrup to the top.

Pasta: Using your fork, separate a few strands. Hold the tip of the prongs against the edge of the plate and twirl the fork around to gather the strands onto it. Don't use a spoon: even in Italy that's acceptable only at a trattoria—a very informal, family-type setting.

CAVEAT: It's so difficult to avoid dripping sauce onto your clothing, or you end up with one strand dangling from your mouth. If you have any choice at all, we recommend that you don't order pasta.

Petits fours (or small cakes): These are finger foods and are eaten in small bites.

How to Handle Inedibles

The simple rule is: take inedibles out of your mouth the same way they were put in. In other words, remove grape seeds with your fingers, because you eat grapes with your fingers; gristle is removed with your fork; pits, such as prune pits, are removed with a spoon.

The only exception is a fish bone. Although fish is eaten with a fork, you remove a fish bone from your mouth with your fingers. Place whatever you are removing at the edge of your plate.

Remember, all the above are guidelines so that you will know how to behave under any circumstances. But if the client picks up the chicken or the lamb chop with his or her fingers by all means feel free to do so, too. Consideration of others and forgetfulness of oneself are of paramount importance in the host/client relationship that you are trying to establish.

Making Wine Selection Simple

For anyone curious about the wines of the world there are any number of wine-tasting courses, as well as a growing library of excellent books on this fascinating subject. We hope you will investigate what's available in your geographic area: learning even the basics about wine can be enormously rewarding.

You don't have to become an expert before you can enjoy wine or encourage your guests to do so. Ordering wines at a business luncheon or dinner may be kept fairly simple.

■ ■ ■

A SUMMARY OF

Do place your napkin in your lap as soon as you are seated at the table.

Do place your napkin on the table to the left of your place if you must leave the table.

Do lean slightly forward each time you take a mouthful of food. If anything drops it will fall into your plate.

Do wipe your lips with your napkin before taking a drink.

Don't wipe your mouth with one hand while holding a knife or fork with the other.

Do keep your free hand in your lap or rest your wrist on the edge of the table.

Do break off a small portion of bread (or roll) over the bread and butter plate, before buttering. Use the bread and butter plate to hold olives, radishes, and other finger foods.
Remember that this plate is not used at a formal dinner.

Do mention if the food has been delightfully served or is especially delicious.

Don't talk about your personal food likes and dislikes at the dinner table.

Do leave your plate where it is when you have finished eating, with the knife and fork in the finished position.

■ ■ ■

If, when the waiter first takes your drink order, your guest asks for a glass of wine instead of whiskey or a cocktail, that's the perfect time for you to suggest that you both might enjoy a bottle of wine with lunch. If the guest agrees, ask for the wine list and tell the waiter to direct the wine steward to your table.

Otherwise, the wine list is usually presented with the menu. The *sommelier*, or wine steward, will suggest a glass of wine or perhaps an *aperitif* (a flavored alcoholic drink taken before the meal to stimulate the appetite).

■ ■ ■

DO'S AND DON'TS

Don't *push your plate away, lean back from the table, and announce, "I'm stuffed."*

Do *remember the "silent service" code of positions for your knife and fork.*

Don't *rest your cutlery half on and half off the plate, like oars.*

Don't *gesture with your knife, fork, or spoon in your hand. If you're not using the utensil, put it down.*

Do *remember food is always on your left, beverages on your right.*

Don't *eat your neighbor's salad. A right-handed person will reach across the dinner plate to eat salad.*

Do *ignore any silverware that may fall to the floor. Pick up the next piece and continue. If there is no other utensil, signal discreetly for the waiter to bring another.*

Special notes to female executives:

Don't *place your purse on the table. It belongs in your lap or in your hand. Even in the finest restaurants, placing a purse next to one's chair or hanging it on the back of the chair is deemed unsafe nowadays.*

Don't *apply lipstick or comb your hair at the table. Excuse yourself and take care of your personal grooming in the ladies' room.*

■ ■ ■

If you and your guest desire wine, inquire about the *house wine*: is it domestic or imported? Is white, red, or blush available? Is it dry or semidry? Can you order a full or half carafe?

House wines are almost always simple, pleasant-tasting, all-purpose wines. Because they are usually moderately priced, they represent good value, too. Unless your guest indicates that something else would be preferable, the house wine is a safe choice. And you really don't have to know anything at all about wine to make that decision!

Which Wine?

Since wine is meant to enhance your enjoyment of food, the wine you choose will depend upon the entrée you've selected. Here's a simple rule to follow:

Drink white wine with fish and poultry, red wine with meat.

If you have trouble remembering which are the white wines, the following mnemonic tricks should make things easy:

CHardonnay (American, pronounced shar-duh-*nay*) and *CHablis* (French, pronounced sha-*blee*) are fine accompaniments for *CH*icken.

SOave (Italian, pronounced *swah*-vay) is good with *SO*le. What about red wines?

BEaujolais (French, pronounced boe-jhoe-*lay*) is a red wine to drink with *BE*ef, as is *Bordeaux* (French, pronounced bor-*doe*) and *Barolo* (Italian, pronounced ba-*roe*-lo).

Usually, the wines served during a meal are described as "dry," which means that they are not sweet. However, champagne is labeled differently: A champagne marked *dry*, or *sec*, is the *sweetest* of sparkling wines. *Extra dry* will be a bit less sweet. The driest champagnes are labeled *brut*.

The sommelier will be happy to advise you. By all means, rely upon his or her expertise—he knows the restaurant's wine cellar as well as the best choices of wine for the foods you've ordered. Let the wine steward do his job for you.

Sommelier (sum-el-*yay*) comes from the French word

somme, and refers to the carriage that contained the king's food and drink when he went on a journey. The sommelier's job was to taste the food and drink prepared for the king to make sure they were not poisoned.

Exercise Restraint

In the headiness of the moment resist the temptation to use your expense account to order any famous—exorbitantly priced—wine you may have read or heard about. Research has shown that this sends a negative message to the client: "Oh, am I going to make lots of money off you!"

You'll appear frivolous, if not a bit pretentious, and somewhat disloyal to the firm whose money you're squandering.

Also, the client may infer that you're trying to bribe or impress him. No one wants to suspect that his or her favor is being purchased for the price of a bottle of wine, even if it is Château Lafite-Rothschild.

Save the expensive wines for in-house celebrations, *after* you've landed the account!

When the Wine Is Served

The wine steward's practice of presenting the bottle, uncorking it, and pouring the wine for the host is no arcane ritual, but a sequence of logical steps.

The bottle of wine is presented to you so that you can be certain it's exactly what you ordered. Look at the label. Is it the vintage you wanted? The château or winery?

The steward will remove the cork and hand it to you. Squeeze it. Is it moist or dry? A dry cork indicates that the bottle was not stored on its side; oxygen may have entered the bottle and affected the taste of the wine. Smell the cork—is the aroma pleasant, or vinegary and sour? If the cork is moist and sweet-smelling nod to the sommelier to proceed.

After placing the cork on the table, the steward will pour a small amount of wine into your glass. There are two reasons for this: you'll be able to sniff the wine to determine whether it smells sour, and if any pieces of

A Typical French Wine Label

MOUND HILL

"HOUSE"
FUMÉ BLANC
(SAUVIGNON BLANC)

1986 NAPA VALLEY

CELLARED & BOTTLED BY
MOUND HILL VINEYARDS, SAN REMO, CALIF.
ALCOHOL 12.9% BY VOL.

A Typical American Wine Label

the cork have broken off, they will fall into your glass and not your guest's.

In ancient times, the host sipped the wine first to prove to his guests—frequently rival chieftains—that it was safe to drink.

Look at the wine in your glass. See that the color is clear and sharp. Swirl it gently in the glass; then smell it. You should be able to detect the wine's bouquet, or fragrance. Now, sip it. How does it taste? Does it taste vinegary? Or is it smooth? If so, put the glass on the table and nod your approval to the sommelier, who will then pour the wine for your guest(s). Your glass is filled last.

Wine lovers are fond of saying that wine is a living thing until it has been drunk. Certainly the flavor continues to deepen in your glass, as the wine "breathes"—comes into contact with the air. That's why wineglasses are never filled to the rim. The air in the bowl of the glass helps to bring out the full flavor of the wine.

Sip the wine throughout your meal. The steward or the waiter should be alert to refill your glasses whenever necessary.

■   ■   ■

The Toast originated during the Middle Ages, when people put a piece of scorched bread into a tankard of beer or wine because they thought it improved the drink's flavor. When they realized that the bread had no effect on the flavor of the wine, they eliminated the bread but retained the ceremony of raising the glass to honor someone.

■   ■   ■

Understanding the Wine Label

Whether the wine is European, American, from South America or Australia, the label will tell you everything you need to know about what's in the bottle. The labels on pages 46 and 47 are from wines of France and California. Notice that each tells you:

• the name of the wine.

- the producer—the French château, the California winery
- where the wine comes from
- where the wine was bottled (*mis en bouteille au château*) (bottled at the winery)
- if the wine has achieved a particular status: as
  ### GRAND CRU CLASSÉ/
  ### GOLD MEDAL
- the vintage—only if a specified percentage of the wine is of a particular year. Many well-known, reliable wines are blended of harvests of several years.

"POWER" BREAKFASTS

With the hectic pace of the modern business world, the nine-to-five working day has become a relic of the past. Today's successful executive rises with the sun, and uses the dawn's early light to have a "power" breakfast—so named because of the high-caliber executive presence at so many of those weekday get-togethers.

There are good reasons why many executives prefer to meet for breakfast, rather than lunch:

- The occasion has a built-in time frame: you can't sensibly meet before seven-thirty or go much beyond nine o'clock.
- Since neither wine nor liquor are served, there's no possibility of anyone overindulging.
- Eating lightly, as one can at breakfast, reflects our current concern about healthier food habits.
- The first appointment of the day is an easy one to keep, and it adds flexibility to the schedule. As one busy executive put it, "How many times a week can you go out to lunch? When I have a breakfast meeting, I can use lunchtime to think!"
- Because hotel dining rooms are frequently the only restaurants open for breakfast (we don't suggest you get together at a fast-food outlet or coffee shop), the service is usually first-rate and the tables are set far enough apart to guarantee privacy.
- Last, but certainly important in these cost-conscious

days, breakfast can be a more economical way of entertaining clients.

Keep in mind that a successful breakfast meeting should have a short agenda. Don't try to accomplish too much in those ninety minutes.

Choose your meeting place carefully. At the most popular "in" hotel, you may run into so many people you know that you'll spend the morning shaking hands and saying "Hello" rather than talking with your client.

THE AFTERNOON TEA

As a contrast to the brisk dynamic of the breakfast meeting, consider the unhurried atmosphere of the increasingly popular afternoon tea.

Smart executives and hotel managers are discovering that a lot of business can be done in the quiet afternoon—from about three-thirty until cocktail or dinnertime. Female executives have told us that they feel the setting provides an ideal environment for nurturing a positive business relationship. Can you imagine a hostile meeting over tea? Doesn't an invitation to tea conjure up an aura of reverence for tradition, the expectation of a charming, genteel experience?

Think of the benefits:

- This is the last appointment of the day—no one has to rush back to the office.
- The usually elegant hotel salon offers more privacy than a bustling restaurant at lunchtime.
- As there's only one sitting, you'll never have to wait for a table.
- No alcohol need be served, except possibly a small glass of sherry.
- There's an intriguing element of up-scale propriety associated with afternoon tea that can focus favorable attention on you as being innovative yet respectful.

As always, be sure to make a reservation, confirm with your guest, and reconfirm with the hotel.

CAVEAT: Don't make the mistake of calling this occasion high tea. That term refers to a poor man's supper —it's a contraction of the starving husband's complaint: "It's high time we had something to eat!"

Serving Tea

Afternoon tea consists of a series of courses: never fear that you or your guest will go away hungry.

First, you'll select your tea. There are many varieties—and we suggest you familiarize yourself with them. The most popular are:

- Darjeeling (dahr-*jeel*-ing), a delicate blend favored in the exclusive clubs of London;
- Earl Grey, a fragrant, full-bodied Chinese tea;
- Assam (as-*sahm*), a robust tea from India;
- Orange Pekoe (*pee*-coe), a smooth-flavored Ceylon blend;
- Lapsang Souchong (*soo*-chong), a pungent, smoky tea from China.

Most likely, the *teapot* will contain boiling water and loose tea. Allow the tea to infuse, or mash, for about four minutes before you fill your cup. Place the small *tea strainer* over your cup to collect the "bastard" leaves. After tea has been poured, dump the leaves into the small silver dish, or *slop bowl*, on the table. Rest the strainer on top of the slop bowl. We think it's a nice gesture for the host executive to pour for the guest.

If the tea is too strong, dilute it with hot water from the *other teapot*, which is brought with the tea.

In the event you're served conventional tea bags, there will be only one teapot, filled with boiling water. Put the used tea bags in your saucer, never in the ashtray.

Add small cubes of sugar to taste—"one lump or two?"—with the *silver sugar tongs*.

Tea is traditionally drunk with milk, never cream. Lemon is frequently served as well. Use the small *lemon fork* to pick up the wedge from the china plate.

Next, you'll be offered a tray—or tiered stand—laden with finger sandwiches on firm white, dark, or oatmeal bread. The fillings can range from simple watercress or cucumber and sweet butter to salads and wonderfully hearty meat spreads flavored with mustard and curry. Don't worry about which knife or fork to use: as the name suggests, these are eaten with your fingers.

Sweets follow: Scones and pastries, to be slathered with butter or clotted cream and any one of several kinds of jam.

Scone is an anglicized version of an old Dutch word, *schoonbrot*, which means "beautiful bread." Tea-table etiquette requires that you split the scone in half with the *tea knife*; bring the jam and butter onto the tea plate; spread a little butter on a small, bite-size portion of the scone and top the portion with jam. Do not spread butter and/or jam on the entire half of the scone all at one time.

When clotted cream is served, add globs of it after the jam. In other words, a bite-size piece of scone would be topped with butter, jam, and then cream.

In many hotels, there's still more—your choice of cake,

■ ■ ■

TEA LORE

Drinking tea predates coffee drinking by centuries: The Chinese were drinking tea four thousand years ago. The tea trade has shaped world history. Tea was the favored beverage in the Colonies until the fateful afternoon of December 16, 1773, when Boston's Sons of Liberty boarded the fleet of merchant ships anchored in the harbor and dumped 342 chests of tea overboard, to protest the British tax policy. Dubbed the Boston Tea Party, this incident resulted in even more punitive measures by the British rulers and hastened the Revolutionary War.

We have Anne, the seventh Duchess of Bedford, to thank for the custom of afternoon tea. During the summer of 1840, to allay the dreadful sinking feel that overtook her each afternoon at four o'clock— while waiting for dinner, which wasn't served until eight o'clock—she asked for a tray of tea, bread and butter, and cake to be brought to her room. When the other ladies of the court learned of her secret snack, the habit quickly spread.

■ ■ ■

fruit tarts, or pastry. For dessert lovers, afternoon tea is an inspired addition to the business day.

You may end the occasion with a glass of sherry.

Corporate Teas

A growing number of firms are choosing the corporate tea as a way to entertain staff members as well as clients. The soothing ritual—and comforting food—effectively puts co-workers at ease.

Tea carries the implication that the activity ends early and everyone goes home at a normal hour.

The message is also clear that it's a nonalcoholic occasion. There need be no concern about driving home safely, or about anyone overindulging, except on good food.

INEVITABLE EVENTS

The Cocktail Party

The late afternoon, when you're tired and hungry, is not the best time to have to attend an event where liquor is being served. You're the only one who can judge your physical condition: if there's the slightest possibility that drinking alcohol could present any sort of problem for you, limit yourself to a glass of club soda, and nurse it.

Whatever you're drinking, hold the glass in your left hand. The purpose of a cocktail party is to meet people. You're always shaking hands—it's called "working the room." A glass held in the right hand leads to icy, wet handshakes, which are not appealing.

Just because you love smoked salmon, caviar, or whatever hors d'oeuvres you spy on the buffet table, that's no excuse to pile it on. A perpetually filled plate in your hand comes to look like an extension of you. This is not a substitute for dinner.

Do yourself a good turn. Before you go to the party, drink a glass of milk to coat your stomach and keep you from being ravenous.

It seems one always sees the most attractive people at cocktail parties. But you're there to represent your company. Resist the temptation to flirt. This is not the time or the place. Being so indiscreet is foolish, and shows poor judgment. If you meet someone you absolutely must see again, pursue that relationship on your personal time.

Banquet Behavior

The purpose of a formal corporate banquet is generally to honor an important member or friend of the company. Here's what to do at such occasions.

At a banquet in honor of someone, arrive before the guest of honor and depart only after the guest of honor has left.

Formal seating arrangements call for the male guest of honor to escort the hostess to her seat, but to seat the woman to his right. The man to the left of the hostess is responsible for seating the hostess.

Everyone stands for the first toast, *except* the person being toasted. Nor does that person drink.

If someone proposes a toast in your honor, you neither stand nor drink, but remain seated. You may propose a toast to others present: stand, raise your glass in the air as you make your toast, say a few words about the person(s) you're honoring, and then you may drink.

If you are on the dais or in the audience and are introduced by the chair, stand briefly to let everyone know where you are.

Don't smoke at the table while food is being served.

Don't leave the table or converse during a speech.

Informal Dinners at the Home of Colleagues or Superiors

These invitations are certainly an indication that your work has attracted favorable attention. They present an opportunity to show how well you handle yourself in social situations that may be a bit more intimate than the banquet or cocktail party.

Your conversational skills will come into play—it's your chance to show that you have developed interests beyond your work.

Spouses of married executives will now have a chance to get to know one another, although they are generally not seated together at dinner.

Unmarried executives should not assume that it's all right to bring a friend as a date for the evening. Ask. It's possible that you're expected to be the partner of another guest.

Punctuality is important. An invitation for 6:30-ish means no later than 6:50. Nor should you be the last to leave. Once the most important guests have left, it's time for you to go home.

Let moderation be the key. You want to be able to drive home, and may even be asked to drop off other guests.

Corporate Outings

Events such as the company picnic, boat ride, baseball game, or outdoor concert serve as great opportunities to spend time with colleagues in an extremely relaxed, casual atmosphere. People often reveal unexpectedly winning aspects of their personality when they feel free to act like members of one large, cheerful family.

The informality of the situation is never an excuse to treat the territory with disrespect, however. Ashtrays should be placed strategically throughout the area; if they are not available, smokers must remember to field strip their cigarettes and not toss them carelessly on the grass. Of course, all napkins, paper cups, wrappings, plates, and party paraphernalia should be collected (in oversize bags) and deposited in the appropriate refuse containers.

Follow the advice of the National Park Service: "Leave nothing but footprints, take nothing but photographs."

Lunch as Part of the Job Interview

It's easy to understand why this can be a terrifying situation. Who wouldn't be nervous? After all, so much depends upon how you perform at this meeting.

Of course you want to do well. You want the job. But do you really need to be so fearful? Let's look at the situation.

You've come this far. Obviously you have the necessary qualifications, or you would have been eliminated before this. What will having this lunch do for you?

This meeting is your opportunity to demonstrate your social skills: how charming you can be, how at ease in a public place. Like the executive who wants to establish a relationship with a client, you're going to have the chance to show that your manners are good, that you're bright and energetic and respectful, and that you know how to handle your knife and fork, sip a glass or two of wine, possibly nibble salad and dessert.

We've outlined the progress of the meal, suggested a safe course through the menu, even offered advice on handling foods that may be unfamiliar to you.

Does anyone want you to do badly?

No! The person interviewing you wants you to succeed! The company wants you to be the answer to its prayers: it has a position to fill; it wants to end the tiresome interview process, hire someone, and get on with business. So, you are meeting with someone who is already on your side. All you need do is be as terrific as your résumé and your recommendations have said you are.

How can you help yourself?

Practice. There's hardly an element of this meeting that you can't anticipate: like any actor, you can rehearse. You already know about the company; you can learn more about the executive. You doubtless have an idea of what your job will entail and what you believe you can contribute to the organization. Yes, you can visit the restaurant in advance, and even sample the food. And you can remember that there's a real world out there, too, and be able to talk about what's going on in it.

Is there anything else?

Just make sure your suit is clean and pressed. And relax. You'll be fine.

CHAPTER FOUR

EXECUTIVE ENTERTAINMENTS

"A painter paints his pictures on canvas. But musicians paint their pictures on silence. We provide the music and you provide the silence."
—LEOPOLD STOKOWSKI, REPRIMANDING A TALKATIVE AUDIENCE

T HE GREATER PART OF EXECUTIVE EN-
tertaining takes place at meals of varying levels of
formality. As the relationship flourishes, however, you
may find it desirable, or necessary, to spend time with
clients or co-executives (accompanied by spouses) in more
social situations. An ideal way to accomplish this is to
extend an invitation to attend the theater, a concert, or
the ballet.

AUDIENCE ETIQUETTE

There's a delicious atmosphere of anticipation at any live
performance, no matter whether you're seeing a dance
program, a concert, or play. The auditorium fairly crack-
les with excitement as the audience takes their seats. As
the houselights dim, the tension mounts. Then the lights
go out, the curtain rises, the performance begins, and
we're transported to some other place—a world of sound,
or light, music, dance—a world of the imagination.

Whether you plan to see a colorful musical, an ex-
perimental play in a small off-Broadway or community
theater, a grand opera, a "pop" concert, a classical ballet,
or a program of ethnic dance, here are a few things to
remember.

Getting the Most Enjoyment
from a Performance

To the executive for whom any type of theatergoing is
a new, and possibly unwelcome, experience, the major
challenge of the evening may be managing to stay awake
for two hours. The anxiety of being in such alien territory
can have a sleep-producing effect.

As with a new business project, the first step is to do a bit of homework: familiarize yourself with the material you're going to see or hear. No work of art is ever instantly comprehensible.

Playing the album of a Broadway musical will give you a very good idea of the action; listening to recordings of the ballet music, or the symphony or opera you expect to attend will accustom your ear to the major themes and variations. This awareness of what to listen for is the equivalent of an outline of the evening's agenda. If you're seeing a play, there's always material on what the author has previously written and what this new work signifies. And, one can always read the critics' reviews.

Any information or anecdotes about the composer, writer, the production, or the performers will give you plenty to talk about before and after the performance. Strengthening your involvement in the evening's entertainment should serve to keep you awake.

You can also help yourself by eating lightly before the performance. With curtain time usually at 8 P.M., it would be sensible to opt for a hearty afternoon tea rather than a hurried dinner.

It's also a good idea to avoid drinking alcoholic beverages before the show. Otherwise, that comfortable seat in the warm, dark theater will become the perfect place to relax. You may close your eyes for just a moment and wake up with a start who knows how many minutes later, wondering if you've been snoring.

Buying Tickets

Tickets should always be purchased in advance. The more successful the show, the further in advance you must plan in order to get good seats.

While *orchestra seats*, those on the main floor of the theater or auditorium, are usually the most expensive, they are not always the best seats for every entertainment. For musicals and dance programs, seats in the *mezzanine* or *balcony* will afford you an overhead view of the entire stage, so that you can see the choreographer's patterns. At a concert, almost any location will do, so long as you can hear the music clearly.

If a member of your party is handicapped, is extremely tall, or may conceivably be called to the telephone during the performance, ask the box-office attendant if aisle seats are available.

It is usually possible to order tickets by telephone and charge them to a major credit card. They will then be held in your name at the theater box office; you may pick them up at any time before the show. There may be an additional charge for this service.

CAVEAT: If tickets are merely reserved, or *held in your name*, be sure to ask by what time they must be picked up and paid for. We know of a young executive who arrived at the box office with his party only moments before curtain time, and was exasperated to discover that the tickets being held in his name had been sold to someone who'd been waiting to catch a cancellation or a no-show. Our friend had forgotten that reservations were held only until twenty minutes before curtain time.

To make matters worse, he screamed at the box-office attendant, "No tickets? What do you mean *no tickets*?" to which the woman replied, sweetly, "I'm terribly sorry, sir, which word didn't you understand?"

Arriving at the Theater

The first rule of theater etiquette is to arrive in plenty of time to take your seats and get settled before the show starts. That's a simple indication of respect for the performers and for the people sitting in your vicinity.

At even the most carefully planned modern theater complex there will inevitably be a traffic jam when several hundred people in cars, taxis, and limousines converge at the same place within the same fifteen- or twenty-minute period.

CAVEAT: Late arrivals should not expect to be seated until after the scene or current selection is finished.

It's so much more comfortable to check coats and hats, as well as any personal packages and briefcases, rather than sit with them on your lap throughout the evening. Allow extra time for this, too.

Seating Your Party

The ticket-taker will tear your tickets at the entrance, give you the stubs, and direct you to the usher, who takes your stubs and leads you to your seats. The client (and spouse) follows the usher; the host walks behind them. The usher returns the stubs to the host.

If no usher is available, the executive leads the way to the seats, with the client following.

In this country, ushers are not tipped.

CAVEAT: Always retain your ticket stubs. Computers now print seat locations on your tickets at the time of purchase, and mistakes can occur. We've seen two couples try to occupy the same pair of seats; both held tickets for the identical locations, for the same performance. Luckily, a competent house manager was able to find places for everyone.

When there are two couples in the party, one of the men enters first, followed by the two women and finally by the other man. Traditional etiquette suggests that each woman sits next to the man who is not her spouse or companion. Except in the case of a very tall or handicapped person (as mentioned above), a man—the host— should sit on the aisle seat.

When the party is large, a woman (the wife of the host) leads the way into the row; the others follow in the man-woman alternating pattern.

If other people are already seated in the row, and you must pass them to reach your seats, say, "Excuse me, please." They will either turn their legs to the side or stand to let you through. It is more polite to face those already seated as you make your way through the row.

What About Programs?

A free program is given to every concert-, ballet- or theater goer. Usually the usher hands programs for everyone in the party to the host, who then distributes them to the guests after everyone is seated.

Souvenir programs, which frequently feature biographies and portraits of the principals, stories about the production, and other publicity material, are sold before and after the show and during the intermission. As a gesture of additional hospitality, you may wish to purchase one program per couple.

■ ■ ■

ONE THEATER'S "TEN COMMANDMENTS"

The program booklet for New York's famed Carnegie Hall recently contained a list of "ten command-ments"—rules for audience behavior. Among them were:

Thou shalt not:
talk.
hum, sing, tap fingers or feet.
rustle thy program.
crack gum in thy neighbors' ears.
jangle thy jewelry, or wear loud-ticking watches.
open cellophane-wrapped candies.
snap open and close thy purse.
sigh with boredom.
read (houselights remain on during concerts).
arrive late or leave early.

■ ■ ■

During the Performance

Our enjoyment of a concert, play, or any other enter-tainment depends greatly upon our comfort and our abil-ity to concentrate on the performance. Talking (or prolonged loud whispering) prevents those around you from enjoying the show. Such rudeness is disrespectful to the performers and distracting for the audience.

Audience response, the emotional interaction between the cast and the audience, is what makes a live perfor-mance different from any other entertainment. The per-formers are nourished by the sense that the audience is paying attention. Actors will frequently say that each audience is different, and so every live performance is different from the others because of the unique chemistry of this interaction.

For many new theatergoers, the temptation to talk back to the characters, particularly at moments of emo-tional crisis in the plot, is frequently difficult to control. Theater professionals refer to the proscenium—the arch at the front of the stage which separates the playing space from the auditorium—as the *fourth wall*. It creates the boundary, the necessary aesthetic distance, between the players and the audience. This invisible wall enables us to peek at the action, to be a part of the life unfolding onstage, without infringing on it. The wall is like a gigantic TV screen through which one watches the performance but doesn't participate in the action.

Laugh at the humorous lines and funny situations; gasp at the surprises and weep at the tragic moments. Just don't talk out loud to your neighbor—or to the cast.

Dealing with Talkers

Some people seem oblivious to the fact that their talking is annoying to the people around them. If meaningful glances haven't been effective in getting their attention, you may touch the talker gently and say quietly, with a bit of a smile, "Excuse me, I'm having difficulty hearing the performance."

If the talker's seated behind you, turn around and softly say the same thing.

Amorous Couples

Deep affection and/or physical attraction should not be displayed in public. Lovers who need to hold each other close or keep their heads together make it impossible for anyone seated behind them to see the stage. Deal with them as you would with talkers: Touch one on the shoulder and whisper, "I can't see if you keep your heads together."

About Refreshments

Eating during a performance is annoying. After all, is there a real danger that you will die of starvation before the final curtain?

Candies, fruit drinks, and other refreshments are sold during intermission, and should be consumed only during that period.

In the days of radio drama, sound effects men crinkled pieces of cellophane in front of the microphone to simulate the roar of a forest fire. Crinkling candy wrappers during a performance can be as distracting as loud conversation.

Do's and Don'ts of Applause

While we disagree with those who insist that television is to blame for everything that's wrong with modern civilization, it does seem that decades of televised sports events and game shows have legitimized one peculiar aspect of American audience behavior—the willingness to clap hands for no reason.

American audiences applaud the curtain rising on an empty set, the entrance of almost any character, and, at revivals of hit shows, they applaud the introductory notes of songs they remember from the original production!

Applause, like a promotion or a bonus, is a way of showing appreciation for a job well done. Of course, there are exceptions.

At a concert
Do applaud when the conductor enters and takes his or her place upon the podium.

Do applaud at the end of a complete work.

Don't applaud between movements of a symphony or after a solo.

At a ballet
Do applaud when the conductor enters.

Do applaud after a *pas de deux* (French, pronounced pah-duh-*dooh*, means a duet) or a solo.

Do applaud at the end of the complete work.

At the theater
Don't applaud entrances, even the star's.

Don't applaud the empty set when the curtain rises.

Do applaud at the end of a scene or act.

Do applaud the working of a particularly intricate bit of stagecraft—such as the appearance of the gondola floating through the fog in *Phantom of the Opera*.

Do applaud a performer who has exited after a great scene.

Don't applaud the introduction to a song you happen to like or know.

Do applaud at the end of a song or dance.

At the opera
Do applaud when the conductor enters.

Do applaud at the end of an aria.

Do applaud at the end of the act when the performers take their bows.

SPORTS ETIQUETTE

Sporting events are among our oldest rituals. Nowadays, when so many of us are ardent sports fans or dedicated participants, attending these events is a fine way to communicate on common ground, forge strong relationships, and have fun. Many modern companies sponsor softball games or squash tournaments, or offer tickets to sporting events to reward employees who are performing well.

As we advised the novice theatergoer, take some time to learn the fundamentals of any game you expect to watch or play. Nothing spoils the enjoyment or the rhythm of the game so much as having to explain what's going on, or wait while a newcomer (you) figures out that it's his or her turn to do or say something.

Spectator Sports

If tickets are necessary, be sure to obtain them in advance. Try to get a map of the stadium, arena, or track, so you have some idea of where your seats are in relation to the parking facilities.

This is an ideal occasion to avoid the entire parking hassle by reserving a limousine.

Finding Your Seats

As at a theatrical event, your ticket will be torn at the entrance and you'll be directed to your seat section, where an usher will take your stub, find your place, flip the seat down, and dust it for you.

It is customary to tip the usher for this service. A dollar a couple is sufficient.

To Scream or Not to Scream

Electronic scoreboards are intended to encourage crowd noise. So you might just as well join in and do your best to spur your team to victory. Of course, that doesn't give anyone permission to yell incessantly or to shout insults at the opposing players.

If you're seated near one of these boors, you may ask courteously that they "Keep it down to a roar, please."

In certain cities, fans have been known to bring radios and/or televisions to the stadium so that they can keep up with other games (or perhaps learn the details of the one they're attending). Avoid adding more noise to the roar by using headphones or the earplug speaker.

At sports requiring intense individual concentration —such as golf, tennis, or backgammon—commonsense as well as common courtesy dictates that no spectator (or player) do anything to create a disturbance that might possibly derail a player's attention.

When the action really gets exciting, and the entire audience seems to rise almost as a unit, try to remember that everyone behind you wants to see what's going on just as much as you do. If you ask politely, the people in front of you won't mind sitting down so that you have a view of the action.

Just be sure you don't cause anyone to yell, "Down in front!"

Playing the Game

Good sportsmanship—which has been defined as grace under pressure—is essential to an executive's character. To many people, sports behavior is a metaphor for business behavior. Both require courage, alertness, determination, and a degree of ruthlessness.

The late football coach Vince Lombardi told his players that "Winning isn't everything, it's the only thing."

Chris Evert Lloyd has a different view: "If you can react the same way to winning and losing, that's a big accomplishment. That quality is important because it stays with you the rest of your life, and there's going to be a life after tennis that's a lot longer than your tennis life."

A player with good sports manners:

- is always on time, and never holds up anyone's play.
- is appropriately dressed and has the proper equipment.
- knows the rules of the game.
- obeys the rules and never cheats.
- is honest about his or her proficiency or ability.
- doesn't complain about the way a partner or opponent plays.
- loses or wins with equal grace.
- uses no foul language and displays no temper.
- is neat in the changing room.
- treats the playing ground with care.

- pays friendly side bets and wagers immediately.
- shakes hands with everyone at the end of the game, compliments their play, and thanks them for including him or her in the game.

ETIQUETTE AT A PRIVATE CLUB

An excellent way to entertain clients and colleagues is to invite them to one's club. After the game (tennis, golf, billiards, or whatever) guests customarily stay on for drinks and dinner or lunch.

All the rules of good sportsmanship listed above apply in this situation. Everyone pays particular attention to the playing areas, treating the premises with utmost care and respect.

Tennis players should bring at least one unopened can of brand-new tennis balls.

Guests invited to play golf should expect to pay the greens fee and their own caddy fee. As member/host you will sign for all of the other costs. If the member/host signs for the greens fee, the guest should then pay both caddy fees, even if the host protests.

If You're the Guest

An invitation to a private club is particularly gratifying in that it conveys a high degree of personal acceptance and camaraderie. If the club happens to have a colorful history and fine reputation, there's an added element of prestige. Such organizations are frequently housed in impressive quarters: elegant mansions that were once palatial single-family residences, buildings of architectural significance, possibly with landmark status.

Guests who may wish to explore the club premises, or use such member facilities as the library or the lounge, should do so only if they're escorted by the member/host. Historically, a gentleman's club is his home away from home; visitors should not wander about any more than they would explore their host's private home unescorted.

Exclusionary Clubs

One should not invite guests to a place where they will receive less-than-equal treatment.

Female executives who are invited to lunch at men's clubs, and then learn that they must use a special entrance or staircase or elevator, resent it. They reason that they are going to the club for the same business purpose as the male executive who invited them, and feel they shouldn't be discriminated against.

CHAPTER FIVE

COMMUNICATING
EFFECTIVELY

*Our major obligation is not to mistake
slogans for solutions.*
—Edward R. Murrow

T HINK OF EFFECTIVE COMMUNICATION as a great game of tennis. Getting your idea across is like hitting the ball over the net into the other person's court, or consciousness. That person then tries to return the ball to you, with some additional spin—questions, interpretations, contradictions. And so it goes, back and forth, until you reach the end of the game—an understanding.

Communication is *personal*: a dynamic, frequently emotional interaction that involves two or more people. You cannot do it by yourself, any more than you can play tennis alone.

NONVERBAL SIGNALS

The skillful opponent has learned to judge, almost before you've completed your swing, whether your ball will land in the court or out of bounds. You tell him—by the way you place your feet in relation to the net.

That's equivalent to the impression others receive about you, even before you speak. This *nonverbal communication* is what Julius Fast described when he wrote the book *Body Language* in 1970. The way we move all or part of our body communicates an emotional message to the outside world.

Women have historically responded much more openly to these nonverbal messages with reactions like "I don't trust so-and-so, he seems shifty-eyed to me." Often their reactions were belittled as mere feminine intuition. Now we realize they were reacting to nonverbal signals. And they may often have been right.

What messages does your body language convey about you?

Do you let the world know that you're healthy and sure of yourself by standing tall? Or do you slouch and lean against doorways or furniture as if you don't have the energy, or confidence, to stand alone?

Can you stand comfortably with your hands by your side? Or do you keep your hands in your pockets? Are your arms usually crossed in front of you? This involuntary gesture suggests that you're guarding yourself against any possibly disconcerting new thought or idea. Is that the message you intend to convey?

If you don't know what to do with your hands, try carrying a good-size note book or pad. This prop may help relieve your tension and allow you to project a more professional, attentive attitude.

The person with a perpetual frown seems constantly unhappy or disapproving, yet may simply need to wear glasses, or find an effective way to relax and be rid of tension.

Anyone unable to make eye contact can appear deceitful or shifty. This is one of the most difficult habits to modify. One solution is to make eye contact at least at the moment when you begin to speak, and then look into the other person's eyes when you are *listening*.

Once you become aware of the signals you're sending, you can begin to change them if necessary. It's possible to walk briskly, rather than shuffle; to stand erect instead of slouching. You can practice an interested expression instead of a scowl. You can sit up straight instead of sprawling. You can stop scratching your nose, tugging at your hair, drumming your fingers, or whatever it is you do that detracts from a positive perception of you.

HEARD BUT NOT SEEN: TELEPHONE MANNERS

Outside of secretarial schools, proper use of the telephone is never taught. Yet it is second only to the personal business meeting in terms of its importance in the business world.

Making a Call

Before asking for the person you wish to speak to, always identify yourself and your company. For example: "Hello, this is Doris Morgan of XYZ Pharmaceuticals. May I speak to David Westcott?"

Try to cultivate a clear telephone voice. You may want to try a technique used by announcers, smiling while you talk on the telephone. Your voice will be brighter and pleasanter.

Practice speaking slowly and distinctly. The person you're talking to has never heard what you're going to say, even though you may have said the same things many times before. When repeating old information, many of us tend either to rush our words or to mumble, as if the material had ceased to be important or interesting to us. That makes it difficult to understand what you say.

Always identify yourself—even though you may have spoken to this client, or secretary, hundreds of times. It's unrealistic to expect people to guess who you are or recognize your voice. It wastes business time, and gets the conversation off to a poor start.

When the person you're calling answers the telephone, introduce yourself once more, giving your first and last name in case your name was given incorrectly. Do not presume that you are on a first-name basis; the person you're calling must give you permission to use first names. For example: "Hello, Doris. Call me David. What can I do for you?"

If you expect that the call may take a long while, it's courteous to mention this at the start and ask whether another time would be more convenient. Any unexpected call is an interruption of that person's day. As an intruder, you either want permission to continue with what you have to say, or you need to know when it would be better to have this conversation.

If the executive you want to reach isn't available, be sure the person receiving your call understands your name. Give the reason for your call and a time and place (with telephone number) where you can be reached.

Wrong Numbers

You have interrupted someone's day. It is your mistake, after all. The appropriate remark is: "I'm very sorry. I've reached the wrong number. Please excuse the call."

Answering the Telephone

A person answering a telephone for a company, such as a switchboard operator or receptionist, should answer with the company name, stated cheerfully and clearly: "XYZ Pharmaceuticals, Good morning/afternoon!"

For anyone who answers the telephone hundreds of times a day, it can become difficult to maintain that cheerful tone. Yet, as the first representative of the company to the outside world, the telephone receptionist is most important in projecting the company image. A number of corporations have thought to install mirrors at the switchboard, so that the operators can see themselves and be sure they smile when they say "Good morning." It makes a difference.

When answering your own phone, always state your name: "David Westcott [here]."

A colleague's telephone should be answered: "David Westcott's desk, Joan York speaking," or "David Westcott's line, Joan York speaking."

If you share an extension, answer by saying: "Sales Department. Joan York."

If a secretary or colleague has found out who's calling and relayed that information, it's correct to greet the caller by name: "Hello, Doris. This is David Westcott. How are you today?"

An executive may want calls screened. His or her secretary or assistant should ask: "Whom shall I say is calling?"

If the person asked for isn't available, the one answering the telephone should say something like: "Mr. Westcott is meeting with the marketing director. May I take a message for him please?"

Asking a Caller to Wait

It's never appropriate to say, "Hold on," and put a caller on hold. If the person called is speaking on another line, the caller should be *asked* if she/he wishes to hold: "Mr. Westcott's on another line. May I place you on hold?"

The caller may be unable to hold for any number of reasons, and may therefore say: "Please tell him Doris Morgan called. I'm on my way to the convention in Seattle. I'll call him next Tuesday when I return."

If a caller agrees to wait, it's most important to keep that person informed (and not listening to "piped-in" radio commercials or music). Cut in regularly, saying: "I'm sorry. He's still on another line. Would you care to continue to hold?"

You should also offer the caller the option of leaving a message rather than holding on for what may seem an eternity.

We've all been in this position and know the frustration. It takes only seconds to relieve a caller's anxiety. Yet this simple show of consideration—this *un*common courtesy—communicates a caring management style, and can make a significant difference in the way a company and its executives are perceived by outsiders.

Taking Messages and Returning Calls

If you're in a meeting and do not wish to be disturbed, the person answering your calls should say: "Mr. Westcott is in a meeting. May I have him return your call?"

If you're away from your desk and cannot be found, the caller should be told: "Mr. Westcott is in a meeting. May I have him return your call?" rather than: "I'm sure he's around here some place."

The message should give the caller's name, company, and telephone number, and, if necessary, the best time to return the call.

It's extremely discourteous and poor business practice not to return telephone calls within twenty-four hours. Yet the failure to return calls is one of the most common business complaints.

Even an executive who is out of town should check in with his or her assistant and instruct the assistant as to how to return the calls.

Losing Calls

When a telephone call is accidentally disconnected, it's the caller's responsibility to redial. This is simple logic —the caller knows where he or she is calling from; the receptionist, the secretary, or the executive does not.

Disconnects often occur when we try to transfer calls. One way to minimize the potential confusion is to tell the person whose call you are trying to transfer: "If we get disconnected, the person to ask for is . . ."

Yes, if you're the one who somehow touched the wrong button, and you're the one who cut the client off in mid-sentence, then you should be the one to call back and make a joke about clumsiness, gremlins, or whatever you can think of to apologize.

Long-Winded Talkers

You're alone in the office, all of your telephone lights are blinking, but your important client has a lot to say. Is it proper to interrupt a long-winded talker?

Of course. Tell the truth: "Mr. Jones, I'm alone in the office at the moment. May I place you on hold so that I can handle this call on my other line?"

Handling Interruptions

If someone comes into your office while you're on the telephone, say, "Excuse me one moment, please."

Press the mute button, or cover the mouthpiece, respond to the person present, then say to the person on the phone, "I'm sorry," and go on with your conversation.

On the other hand, if a phone call interrupts while someone is in your office, explain to the caller that you're in the midst of a meeting and arrange to return the call later. It's rude to conduct a long telephone conversation in front of a visitor unless it directly relates to the business at hand.

Speakerphone Etiquette

Always ask permission of the person you're talking to to turn on the speakerphone. And identify the people in the room as well: "Harry Brown and Barbara Johnson are here with me, and I know they'll be interested in hearing this as well."

Or, you may be taking notes: "I'm alone in the office and I've turned on the speakerphone so I can write as you talk to me."

Failure to show this consideration to the people you deal with sends a less-than-flattering message about you.

Answering-Machine Etiquette

Companies of all sizes now use answering machines, either on the main switchboard or in special departments.

■ ■ ■

WHO'S MINDING YOUR TELEPHONE?

Whether yours is a service business, heavy equipment manufacturing company, or a chemical plant, every phone call means the same thing: business.

Homebound due to a sprained ankle, the manager of a highly visible service company phoned his office for the day's messages.

He was not happy when the phone rang fifteen times before anyone answered, or that the switchboard operator said the company name so rapidly he wasn't certain he'd dialed the right number.

Wondering if that could be standard practice, he phoned again, this time pretending to be a potential customer. He was immediately placed on hold for four minutes, and then disconnected. On his next phone call he was transferred to four people, none of whom gave him their name. Only two asked his name or the name of his company, or the estimated size of his order. The people he spoke to did not seem to know—or else were unwilling to divulge—the prices of what he was trying to buy.

One employee answered the phone with, "And what's your problem?"

After this painful lesson in what it was like to be a customer, the manager hobbled into his office the next morning to remind the staff:

• A phone should be answered by the second ring; the third ring at the latest.

• When you pick up a telephone, identify yourself.

• Find out who's calling.

• This is your only chance to "meet" the client.

• It's conceivable that the person you just spoke to was impolite, unfair, possibly insulting. That call is now history. You're dealing with a new caller, who should not be the object of your displaced anger.

• The person who's calling evidently wants to buy what we are trying to sell. That person deserves your attention, your consideration, and your respect. If you're not generous with all three, that person will find someone else—one of our competitors—who is.

• Remember that you represent the quality of this company in everything you do.

■ ■ ■

Many people find it disconcerting to be instructed to talk to a machine; they telephoned because they wanted to speak to a real person. Conceivably this may create a negative impression.

On the other hand, answering machines mean that your call doesn't have to be dialed again. Many executives have told us they consider the opportunity to leave a clear, concise message about the nature of their product or service almost as valuable as talking directly to the person they were seeking. And they enjoy the fact that they needn't worry about being interrupted.

Cute messages involving jokes, fake voices, or eerie sound effects are inappropriate in the business world. The outgoing message should give some indication of when the call will be returned, and remind the caller to give his or her name, affiliation, phone number, and a brief message. A considerate caller will respond in kind.

CAVEAT: Announcement-only messages are frustrating; they tell us what we already know—that no one is there to receive our call—and don't allow us the courtesy of leaving the equivalent of a business calling card.

FACE-TO-FACE

American business runs on meetings. Whether it's a small staff meeting or a large corporate conference—and there are hundreds of thousands of those each year—a successful meeting will depend upon the good manners of everyone present.

Good Manners Begin at the Top

A considerate chairman will give sufficient advance notice of a meeting (two weeks, if possible), will schedule the meeting for a time when everyone present can do his/her best (not on Friday afternoons or before important holidays), and will distribute the agenda well in advance, so that attendees have time to think about what they're going to contribute to the discussion.

The well-mannered young executive is expected to:

• arrive on time, homework done, prepared to participate.

- wait until senior executives are seated before taking a chair.
- take careful notes during the discussion (and neither doodle nor twist the paper clips), refrain from interrupting whoever has the floor, thinks before he or she speaks, sticks to the subject, and tries to be sensitive to the dynamics of the group.

Everyone is expected to be mindful of the fact that a meeting is not a signal to smoke cigars or pipes.

Proper Introductions

Despite the fact that they are everyday occurrences in business, introductions can be nerve-wracking for those who have not mastered the skill. The rules, however, are completely logical:

The person of authority, the more important person, is mentioned first.

Clients, senior executives, distinguished guests, or high-ranking dignitaries can be considered authority figures, or persons of importance. You introduce people to them.

So, to introduce Robert Smith, who is your boss, and John Miller, who is your friend, you say: "Mr. Smith, may I present Mr. Miller," or "Mr. Smith, this is John Miller."

It'll be easy if you just remember to say the senior-ranking person's name first, as: "Mr. Smith—[then fill in with some variation on "I'd like you to meet" or "May I present"]—Mr. Miller."

As they say in the entertainment business, "The bigger star gets top billing."

CAVEAT: Even though you may be on a first-name basis with your boss, never call him or her by his or her first name when an "outsider" is present. Always let the boss take the lead, as: "Call me Bob."

Business rules follow social rules. In social situations you would defer to an older person and introduce a younger one this way: "Mr. Seventy, may I present Ms. Thirty." This politeness is shown even if you happen to be presenting your thirty-year-old boss to your seventy-year-old friend.

It's not appropriate to limit yourself to stating the names of the people you are introducing. "Mr. Miller, Mr. Smith; Mr. Smith, Mr. Miller," is hardly satisfactory.

Sometimes the introducer points first to one person and then the other. As they already know who they are, this communicates little more than the nervousness and inadequacy of the speaker.

Nor should you command people in introductions: "Mr. Smith, shake hands with Mr. Miller," or "Mr. Smith, meet Mr. Miller."

To avoid the "Ping-Pong" effect, remember that when you introduce people you need only say their names once.

Don't bounce the names back again in reverse order: "Mr. Miller, Mr. Smith."

Assuming that Mr. Miller has been paying attention, he will have heard you present him to Mr. Smith.

Smoothing the Way to a Conversation

Visitors to Washington, D.C. are often impressed by the deftness with which people in politics handle introductions. The introducer always includes a meaningful nugget of information, which explains the importance, or uniqueness, of the people he or she is bringing together.

Try to follow that example. Include a conversational clue in your introduction. It might be something as simple as: "Mr. Smith, I'd like you to meet Mr. Miller. John and I worked together at XYZ Corporation. He was in charge of quality control," or "John, like you, is an avid skier."

Your conversational clue can provide a basis for their opening conversation.

Difficult Names

Making sure that you pronounce a person's name correctly—particularly if it's an uncommon, or difficult name—shows respect and consideration. It's not only appropriate, it's flattering to ask: "I'm not sure if I know how to pronounce your name properly. What's the correct way to say it?"

Never be so insensitive as to say: "How'd you get a name like that?"

Conversely, if you know you have a difficult name, help the person who's trying to pronounce it. Try to create an association that will make it easier for people to say your name correctly: "It's Sho-sta-KOE-vitch. Like the composer."

If someone mispronounces your name, correct the person gently, and try to make an anecdote of it: "You won't believe this, but I have a list in my office of forty ways to pronounce my name, but the correct way is . . ."

Forgetting Names

It happens to all of us. We look straight into the face of someone we've met before, we can remember the time, the place, and even the sense of the previous meeting, but we cannot for the life of us remember who that person is! What can you do to avoid embarrassment?

The best thing is to be calm and straightforward. "I remember meeting you, but I simply cannot recall your name."

We think it's a bit better to say something like "I'm having trouble recalling your name," rather than the blunt "I've forgotten your name," which may give the impression that the person wasn't important enough to remember.

A former client tells us he uses computer terminology: "I was positive I'd stored your name in my memory, but I am obviously having difficulty retrieving it." He considers this a subtle, amusing way of reminding everyone in the conversation that we are not machines, after all, and we are allowed to make mistakes.

If, on the other hand, you sense that the other person cannot come up with your name, be considerate and rescue that person: "Hi, I'm George Whitman. We met at the Florida session."

Don't, under any circumstances, give hints, such as: "It starts with a W." You're not playing a name game.

Group Introductions

If you are introducing your client to the group, the client is still the figure of authority: "Mr. Client, may I present the members of our sales staff."

When you introduce a new colleague to the group, the

order changes: "Ladies and gentlemen, I'd like you to meet our new colleague, Mr. Green."

Even better would be to act as escort and introduce the new person to each individual in the group.

When Introductions Are Unnecessary

If you're walking with a group and happen to meet someone you know coming from the opposite direction, you're not required to introduce this person to your colleagues. If you stop to chat, the group should continue walking slowly until you finish your brief discussion and catch up.

If you're dining with a group and someone you know happens to walk by your table, you're not obliged to introduce that person to the other diners. If you wish to have a brief conversation, step away from the table.

When You Are Introduced

Sociologists use the term "halo effect" to describe the first thirty seconds of a good meeting—when you are introduced to a person who has an engaging smile, a firm handshake, and who appears genuinely delighted to meet you. In those first thirty seconds, we generally make up our mind about that person. We know—we decide—we've met someone who's obviously "on top of it."

Can you create the halo effect for yourself? Of course. If you are being introduced to someone:

Always rise. Women executives are included in this rule.

Always shake the hand of the person to whom you're being introduced. There's no protocol about who offers whose hand first. We say that the person who offers his or her hand first is the hero. We should all want to be the hero.

Smile cordially and say, "How do you do?" As a memory aid you might repeat the person's name: "How do you do? Mr. Miller."

Save "I'm very glad to meet you" for the times when you are truly sincere—meeting someone you've heard a great deal about, someone whose work has influenced your own, and so forth. Otherwise, "How do you do" is sufficient. Then pick up the conversational clue that the introducer should have provided, and carry on from there.

Speak clearly and distinctly. Look directly into the eyes of the person you are meeting. Give that person the respect of your full attention.

Of course, if you're smart enough to do some homework, and try to learn who you're likely to meet and what they do or have done, you may be able to use those first thirty seconds to even greater advantage.

Using Titles

Professional titles, such as doctor, are used when you're introducing people of unequal rank or age. For example:

A young salesman meeting the founder of the company would be told that the founder was "Dr. Robert Miller."

Official titles, such as governor, ambassador, and congressman are retained even though the person no longer holds that position. So, to introduce your friend to the former governor of your state: "Governor Miller, I'd like you to meet Harry Jones."

Retired service personnel retain their rank. After her retirement from the Women's Army Corps, which she had founded, Oveta Culp Hobby continued to be introduced as Colonel Hobby.

The executive who habitually uses clients' first names, but expects them to address him as Mister or Doctor, is condescending.

Introducing Yourself

When you take the initiative and introduce yourself to someone you don't know, give your first and last names. Don't give yourself a title or honorific. "Hello, I'm Robert Miller," not "Hello, I'm Mr. Miller," and not "Hello, I'm Dr. Miller."

Restaurateurs are always amused by callers who call and announce themselves, "This is *Dr.* Jones. I'd like the large table by the window on Saturday evening. . . ."

The same holds true for messages; you leave your name. Period.

The Professional Woman

A married woman who continues to use her maiden name in business should take pains to see that her husband is introduced by his own name, and not *her* family name. She can introduce both of them.

Jane Pauley, co-anchor of NBC's "Today" show, will say: "I'm Jane Pauley, and this is my husband, Garry Trudeau."

Saying Good-Bye

When you leave a meeting or party, shake hands with the people to whom you've been introduced and say: "Good-bye, Mr. Miller. I'm very glad to have met you," or "I look forward to seeing you again, Mr. Miller."

When to Shake Hands

The handshake is part of the introduction. Business women as well as men always shake hands (unless there's a physical impediment to doing so) when meeting people.

You should also shake hands when you welcome people into your office, when you happen to run into someone you know outside your office, when you say good-bye, and when another person offers to shake hands.

Customs differ in countries around the world, and Americans shake hands far less than people of other nations. Therefore, always clasp a proffered hand. Be alert. It's humiliating for someone to extend a hand and not have the gesture acknowledged.

How to Shake Hands

Handshakes communicate a nonverbal message about us. Personnel officers tell us how startling it is to meet so many healthy, supposedly intelligent, outgoing executives whose handshakes resemble dead fish. Others barely extend their fingertips—as though they fear catching a disease. At the other extreme, there is the overpowerful knuckle crusher, the up-and-down pumper, and the interminable clasper.

Your handshake should be firm but not crippling and should last about three or four seconds.

Introductions at Dinner Parties

At corporate dinner parties where there are fifty or so guests, two members of the staff should be deputized as pilots. They position themselves at the entry and make sure that each guest who enters the room is brought by one of them to meet the host.

The pilot introduces the guest to the host, and then leads the guest to the bar. If the guest is a newcomer to the organization, the pilot should also introduce the guest to one or two people, so that the stranger becomes part of a conversational group.

Pilots can see to it that the host is not cornered by an old friend or client, but spends more or less the same amount of time with all the guests.

Large Parties

At business-social functions where there are more than fifty guests, the receiving line is the best way to make certain that everyone meets the host(s) and gets to talk with the greatest number of people. Also, badges will help to identify people and make conversation easier.

These are necessary courtesies to guests. People who are unable to find the host at a large party can easily feel that their presence makes absolutely no difference.

Receiving lines should be within the party area, far enough from the entrance not to cause a traffic jam.

Spouses do not stand in the receiving line at a business party. If the guest of honor is accompanied by his or her spouse, the spouse of the host also stands in the receiving line with the visitors.

A female executive who is part of the official receiving line is there for business. Wives of the male executives should not expect to stand with their husbands and be introduced to her.

At very large parties, with several hosts' names, the hosts can relieve each other, so as to help the line move more quickly.

If the receiving line is very long, a guest may leave to get a drink and return to the line. But the glass should be disposed of on a passing waiter's tray by the time the guest reaches the hosts.

Hosts should refrain from drinking when they're meeting guests.

Receiving lines should last long enough for every guest to be able to shake hands with the host(s). After they have greeted the first rush of guests, some hosts may be ill at ease standing at the head of a nonexistent receiving line. Nevertheless, they are expected to postpone mingling with the group until all the guests have arrived.

The Introducer

Like the pilot, the introducer adds to the success and pace of the large party, saying each person's name clearly to the host and then introducing the host to the guest. (This is the only occasion where the double introduction mentioned earlier is good manners.)

While guest and host shake hands, the introducer returns to his or her position and brings another guest forward to meet the host.

Assuming there is more than one host in the receiving line, Host #1 now introduces the guest to Host #2 on his or her right, and they shake hands.

If there are others in the receiving line, the guest will now say his or her name and company to each of those people, who will respond by giving their names, and then shake the guest's hand.

Passing through a receiving line, you say, "How do you do?" and comment on the wonderful party, how pleased you are to be there, to meet the guest, and so forth. If you know something about the guest of honor's accomplishments, you may refer to them: "I was so impressed by your report on the merger proposal. I hope we can talk about that later."

THE ART OF EFFECTIVE SPEECH

Whether we're talking on the telephone, meeting face to face, or sending written messages, we all communicate our ideas, goals, wishes, dreams, thoughts, suspicions, and beliefs by using words. Skillfully chosen words can persuade, encourage, motivate, excite, inflame, soothe, amuse, entertain, or delight a listener or reader.

The English language is generally considered to be the richest in the world, with a galaxy of words capable of conveying the slightest nuance of meaning. A successful executive fully understands the value of a large working vocabulary.

The Precise Word

When Ernest Hemingway's first stories were published in the 1920s and '30s, the economy of his prose attracted attention. He wanted to eliminate descriptive words and rely on dialogue to tell the story. He began or ended his characters' speeches with the same two words: "he said" or "she said."

Hemingway was rebelling against what he considered the showy prose of earlier writers, who made it a point never to use the same descriptive word twice. Their characters would mumble, or cough, or gasp, or whisper, or barely utter a few sentences; they'd speak softly, or loudly, but they would never simply *say* anything.

Such a sparse style of writing is fine for a writer aiming to achieve a literary effect, but as a communication style in the eighties, it indicates a dull or lazy thinker with a narrow frame of reference. Today's successful communicators need to search for the word with the exact shade of meaning to convey the intended message.

Of course, to say what you mean, you have to know what you're trying to say. For example: You open the door to an office, and the person sitting at the desk is someone you were not expecting to see.

Are you: surprised? amazed? astonished? shocked? flabbergasted? delighted? upset? amused?

Whichever word you choose will depend upon who the person is, your relationship, your feelings at that instant, and so forth. You make a decision as to the specific shade of meaning you consider most appropriate to the story you wish to tell about that particular scene or moment.

But if you consistently employ the same one or two words to describe a variety of situations, such as:

> Their CEO had an interesting idea.
> I thought their presentation was interesting.
> My secretary made an interesting comment.

Do you think the second speaker was as interesting as the first one?

Or, how about *nice*? For example:

> I told Harry he did a nice job.
> There's something nice about those people. . . .

Words such as *interesting* or *nice* are simply vague. The person you're talking to still doesn't know what in particular you thought was interesting or nice about the idea, the presentation, the secretary's comment, and so forth. You really haven't said anything.

By limiting yourself to such general "uh-huh" words you fail to communicate any sense of your personality, wit, or intelligence. You seem as blah and uninteresting as your vocabulary.

If it suddenly became illegal to use *nice*, *interesting*, *great*, and *awful*, would you be at a loss for words?

Many frequently used words sound similar but have different meanings. For example, do you know when to use flaunt or flout? When you display your new gold watch, you *flaunt* your wealth. If you park in front of a fire hydrant, you *flout* authority.

There are no rules to observe other than to familiarize oneself with the commonly misused words and avoid making mistakes.

Enlarging Your Vocabulary

The easiest way to increase your working vocabulary is to read good books. You don't have to work your way through *War and Peace*; you can sample the writing of the world's best authors in countless anthologies of short pieces on just about any subject.

If fiction, humor, history, or biography don't interest you, read the literature that relates to your business. The finest thinkers in your field have surely written one or two books on their subject: find them and read them.

Read not only for enjoyment and information, but also for style. When you come across a word that's new to you, write it down; look it up; try to use it in conversation when it's appropriate.

This is not easy to do. However, by beginning modestly you will find that the process of increasing your vocabulary, and thereby enlarging your frame of reference, is immediately rewarding.

Euphemisms

During Queen Victoria's time, *leg* was a taboo word. Proper Victorians said *limb*. While everyone knew that limb meant leg, one word was offensive and the other was not. Even the legs of tables were referred to as limbs. Such substitutions—of inoffensive words for upsetting ones—are euphemisms.

Every period has its own euphemisms. In March 1960, *Look* magazine reported: "PAYOLA . . . doesn't sound as ugly as bribe, but it means the same thing." Until the 1970s, the term *abortion* was never used on daytime TV. A doctor performed an *illegal operation* instead.

Nowadays, funeral directors soothe us by talking of the *slumber room*. A clothing store's customers are *king-size*, not fat, people. Children go to school in order to have a *learning experience*, which may or may not be the same as learning lessons. *Fortune* reports on *inventory shrinkage* instead of shoplifting. We *critique* one another's work, because to say we criticize it may sound too negative.

Euphemisms do have a place in our conversation: we need polite ways of handling sensitive topics. "I'm sorry, we have to let you go," is less painful (to the speaker as well as the listener) than bluntly telling an employee, "You're fired."

However, language, like society, is constantly changing. The phrase that was taboo yesterday may be perfectly acceptable today. For example, it would be unnecessarily prudish to refer to "the powder room," or ask a guest if he or she might need to "wash your hands." Use of such euphemisms makes the speaker seem foolish.

Sometimes euphemisms are employed to deceive, intentionally.

A man will say he *misspoke*. Traveling along the euphemistic road brings us to an older word, *misrepresent*, which was frequently heard in the 1960s and may have been a factor in the consumer awareness movement and the resulting consumer protection legislation. The salesman who misrepresented the attributes of his product *lied* about it. The man who misspoke *lied*, too.

Such cynical manipulation of language inevitably damages the user. Confidence, once breached, can rarely be regained.

Vogue-Words

We all are aware of expressions that seem to burst into style almost magically. One day they're hardly noticeable in conversation, the next, everyone seems to be using them.

Charisma was a vogue-word of the sixties: the Kennedys had it and just about everyone else seemed to need it. The seventies gave us *at this point in time*—which simply means "now"—and *arguably*—for which one can substitute *perhaps*. The latest motion picture, automobile, or breakfast food, *at this point in time*, was *arguably* the best of its kind. People who feared that the word *actually* might be commonplace, used the fancier *in point of fact*.

Humongous, *awesome*, *horrific*, *couch potato*, and *where you're coming from* were vogue-words of the 1980s. We hope that seeing them in this context illustrates how the suddenly stylish quickly becomes cliché.

Because they seem so apt, vogue-words can be as irresistible as peanuts—you can't stop using them. And that's their danger. Once overused, they cease to communicate meaning and begin to clutter your conversation. Then it's time to replace them with other words that more accurately communicate what you mean to say.

Slang and Slurs

In the mistaken attempt to show their colleagues what "regular guys" they are, young executives sometimes lapse into slang. The office is not the place to be a "good buddy," and substituting such words as *broad* for woman, *booze* for alcoholic beverages, or *classy* for elegant is not acceptable.

Using what are loosely known as four-letter words is neither a sign of liberation nor sophistication. It is simply foul language.

Avoiding Jargon

Every occupation has its *jargon*—a specialized vocabulary members use to communicate among themselves. There's nothing wrong with jargon, so long as it's used to convey or clarify information to other members of the same occupation.

But if, for example, you ask your financial advisor whether it would be wise to buy or sell a particular security, and what you hear sounds something like: ". . . a possible correction that may affect the up side, but may last long enough to impact on the down side," that's not information or advice that you can understand, it's jargon.

The language of the 1988 IRS tax forms was so impenetrable—jargon-riddled—that more than 30 percent of IRS employees gave the wrong instructions to taxpayers who consulted them for clarification!

To those of us who want to understand the instructions in a manual accompanying a computer program, technically oriented, computer-literate people, speaking as they do in acronyms—GIGO (garbage in, garbage out), RAM/ROM (temporary versus permanent memory)—and such computer terms as boot, baud, ascii, dos, modem, and fax, seem intent on maintaining an aura of mystery rather than clarifying procedure. Of course, that is not their objective. They are trying to explain how their products work. But they are so accustomed to dealing with people who already understand what they are talking about, that they can no longer differentiate between their own technical knowledge and an average reader's general information.

For their 1985 article on "Management Babble," one executive told *American Heritage*: "I have received memos so swollen with managerial babble that they struck me as the literary equivalent of assault with a deadly weapon."

It's easy to recognize jargon when it's used by someone else. But ask yourself if you use jargon when you try to communicate your ideas. Do you want to make your meaning clear, or are you trying to show that you know the private language? Are the technical words or phrases that you use really necessary to the sense of what you want to say? Could they be replaced by simpler synonyms? Is there a simpler way to get your meaning across?

An executive we know had the habit of reading his speeches to his family. Whenever his wife said something like, "Excuse me, dear, I have to do the laundry," he realized he'd forsaken plain language for jargon. Why not ask a friend in a totally unrelated business to listen to your next speech or read your next report, and see if your thoughts are clearly expressed?

Sixty-Four-Dollar Words

As children, many of us learned that antidisestablishmentarianism was the longest word in the dictionary. We also learned that there was no way to slide antidisestab-lishmentarianism into normal conversation. That may have been an important lesson in selecting words for their meaning rather than their grandeur or length.

We have recently discovered a word that's one letter longer than our childhood friend, above—floccipauci-nihilipilification. It's pronounced: floksy-pawsy-nee-hill-i-pill-i-fi-kayshun. It means: the act of estimating as worthless. And that's what your listeners will do to you if you try to use such pretentious language.

There are alternatives to pretentious words. *Sesquipe-dalian* can just as easily be "long." *Entertaining the possible eventuality that* may be "if." One makes *an objective consideration of contemporary phenomena* or simply "looks at the facts."

Like a woman who insists on wearing all of her jewels to a picnic, using uncommon, polysyllabic words for their own sake is just plain showing off. Trying to prove you're better, or smarter, or more knowledgeable than others is bad manners.

Intrusive Words

"Well, like, he's only going to see us if, like, we can get there, like, before, like three o'clock."

Can you tell from that example what we mean by intrusive words?

Allow intrusive words into your conversation and, like rabbits, they multiply. Pretty soon they're all over the place, and you have to chase them out.

How did they get into your speech in the first place? Possibly you used one as a crutch, to continue talking while you were thinking of what it was you wanted to say.

Here's an example of a double fault: intrusive words and incorrect grammar: "So your Aunt Sarah, she says to me, she says, she says 'What do you have to say for yourself?' So I says to her, I says, I says . . ."

The speaker has made a common error: when we relate a conversation that has taken place, the word to use is *said*.

Mispronunciations and Malapropisms

Harry S Truman, our thirty-third president and the only one of our twentieth-century presidents who did not attend college, was self-educated. Reporters assigned to the White House were surprised when he mispronounced many of the words in his huge vocabulary, although he obviously knew exactly what they meant. Because there were few people of his intellect to chat with when he was a boy in Independence, Missouri, he'd never had the opportunity to hear the words in conversation.

Were he alive today, Harry Truman would no doubt keep a pronunciation dictionary at hand, and refer to it whenever he used an uncommon word.

Sometimes words are pronounced incorrectly because they're not the right words at all. For example, a colleague may say: "Mr. Jones and I had *a very good report*."

What your colleague means to say is *good rapport*. *Rapport* is a French word, which means harmony, and is pronounced rap-PORE.

Your colleague may have heard the word pronounced incorrectly: rapPORT. He may have decided the more familiar word, *report*, was what he heard. And so it goes. That's one of the many ways language evolves, but it's also how improper usage creeps into conversation.

That's how we account for the proliferation of *axe*—the mispronunciation of *ask*. A-s-k is neither a difficult nor unusual combination of sounds. The Phantom of the Opera wears a m*ask*; on the beach, sunbathers b*ask*; a chore may be a difficult t*ask*.

This sort of error suggests inattention to detail.

In his eighteenth-century comedy *The Rivals*, Richard Brinsley Sheridan created an outrageous character he called Mrs. Malaprop. Her name was derived from the French, *mal à propos*, which means "out of place." Mrs. Malaprop continually blundered in her use of words, confusing similar-sounding words, often with ludicrous results. Such mistakes are now called *malapropisms*.

"As headstrong as an *allegory* on the banks of the Nile."

"*Illiterate* him from your memory."

"They chopped off his head, I mean he was *decaffeinated*!"

Amusing though such errors may be, they detract

from our image of the speaker as a serious, intelligent, thinking person in whom we can place our trust or our business.

Avoiding malapropisms is a simple matter: think about what you say, keep a growing file of new words, make sure you know what they mean and how to pronounce them.

■ ■ ■

YOU MAY NEED HELP WITH THESE

breadth:	bred-th	not breth
etc./et cetera:	ett set-er-a	not eck setera
height:	hite	not hite-th
length:	lenggth	not lenth
mischievous:	miss-chi-vus	not miss-chee-vee-us
nuclear:	noo-klee-ur	not nuke-you-lur
often:	off-en	not oft-en
picture:	pik-tchur	not pitcher or pik-shur
strength:	strenggth	not strenth
anyway:	anyway	never anyways

■ ■ ■

YOUR SPEAKING VOICE

In the movie classic *Singin' in the Rain*, the late Jean Hagen played a glamourous movie star—"Queen of the Silents"—with a voice so dreadful her co-star, played by Gene Kelly, never permitted her to speak in public. When "talkies" burst upon the screen, the studio executives decided that their next epic, currently being shot, must be a talking picture. But, as they listened to the first day's scenes, the moguls realized that their goddess had the whiny, strident, nasal voice of a Coney Island floozy! Disaster! Heads would roll! The studio would go bankrupt! Careers would be ruined! To the rescue came Gene Kelly, with the brilliant idea that Debbie Reynolds's lovely speaking voice could be recorded on the sound track instead. (Nowadays, that much-used technique is known as "dubbing.") The studio is saved! On to a happy ending.

Do you sound as good as you look? Or are you, like

■ ■ ■

SOME FREQUENTLY USED
FOREIGN WORDS:

au gratin (prepared with cheese and bread-crumbs): oh gra-tanh

Beaujolais (French dry wine, usually red): boh-zho-lay

brut (driest Champagne variety): broot

challis (wool or cotton fabric with a small pattern): shall-ee

champignons (mushrooms): sham-peen-yawnh

Chardonnay (American white wine): shar-d'nay

chic (stylish): sheek

chez (at the home of): shay

concierge (hotel's social events information person): kon-see-airzh

espresso (strong black coffee): ess-press-so

fruits de mer (sea food): froo-wee duh mare

gnocchi (dumplings): nyaw-kee

hors d'oeuvres (appetizers): ore-derv (neither S is pronounced)

prix fixe (fixed price): pree feeks

ragout d'agneau (lamb stew): ra-goo da-nyoe

savoir faire (sophistication): sah-vwahr fare

vin (wine): vanh

■ ■ ■

the glamorous movie queen, totally unaware of the vocal impression you make? The sound of your voice is as important to successful communication as the quality of your handshake and the variety of your vocabulary.

A good speaker knows how to sound confident, authoritative without being strident, sincere, relaxed, emphatic, or soothing, when necessary. A good speaker avoids monotony by varying pace and volume, according to the meaning of the text. A good speaker sounds like an educated person of the area, who pronounces words clearly and distinctly and is easy to listen to and understand.

It is commonly accepted by broadcasters, teachers of forensics, and others in the communication business that Ronald Reagan has provided us with the best example of effective speech since Franklin D. Roosevelt was in the White House. These evaluations have nothing to do with politics, they have to do with getting one's point across. As John Corry, of the *New York Times* said, "His voice is his great weapon. It is not an orator's voice . . . Mr. Reagan does not speak to audiences: he speaks to individuals."

We can hear additional examples of effective speaking every time we turn on the radio or TV: listen to the network announcers and news anchors. Pay attention to their impeccable pronunciation, vocal variety, and fine timing. You can learn to do as well.

Ways to Improve Your Speech

If you don't own a portable cassette recorder, ask a friend if you can borrow one—not to listen to other people's recordings but to hear yourself. (Most people don't recognize their own voices.)

Start by reading aloud into your tape recorder. Begin with a paragraph or a page at a time. Stand when you read; then try sitting or lying down. Notice how changing position affects your tone, your pace, and your pronunciation.

How do you think you sound best?

Once you become accustomed to the sound of your voice, try to isolate the qualities that you like as well as those you want to improve: if you are nervous; if you can't control your breath through an entire sentence; if your voice is nasal, whiny, or raspy and you don't know how to correct it; if you lisp; if you can't say certain sounds—such as *r*, *l*, or *w*—by all means investigate the possibility of getting help. Local colleges may offer evening extension courses in public speaking.

Serious problems deserve the attention of a trained pathologist. Your local hospital may have speech therapists on staff, or may be able to direct you to pathologists who belong to the American Speech, Language, and Hearing Association.

If the thought of speaking to a group fills you with terror—as it does more than 40 percent of the public— you need the help of a communications specialist or of corporate communication consultants whose firms will be listed in the business telephone directory.

Better Voice Means Better Performance

Improving the way you speak reaps additional benefits. Your posture improves, because you notice how much better you sound when you stand (or sit) straight and tall. As you begin to enjoy the sound of your voice, you may also feel more secure about choosing new words to match your better self-image. Enriching your vocabulary makes you a better conversationalist and enables you to express your ideas more effectively.

There is no mystery to becoming an effective speaker. The process is very much like learning to handle oneself at a formal banquet: you practice using the utensils until you're so familiar with them you can forget about the mechanics of the meal and just enjoy yourself.

In the same way, isolating the essential components of effective speech, and mastering them through practice, will free you from anxiety and self-absorption. Then you can be that rarest of creatures, a good listener—one who evaluates what is said, and responds appropriately.

That's an effective communicator.

WRITTEN COMMUNICATION

We don't intend to show how to write inter-office memos or standard business letters, but rather to focus on those special occasions that call for an appropriate written communication.

For example, all of us are ready, willing, and able to send a thank-you letter in response to the lovely "yes" of a signed contract, or the affirmative-sounding "let's see" of a productive meeting. But the talent to send a thank-you letter after the person you've met with has said no will single you out as an exemplary businessperson.

In business, "no" merely signifies, "not today." That doesn't negate the possibility of reconsideration tomorrow. It's even possible that the person to whom you made your presentation today may move to another company tomorrow. And, since it's in that person's best interests to retain contacts and leads, you're sure to be remembered for your professional manner.

Here's one way to say "Thank you for saying no":

Dear Ms. Jones:

Thank you for taking the time to speak with me today. I can appreciate the constraints of a busy schedule. If, in the future, you should decide to customize your product line, please do not hesitate to contact me. I shall be pleased to provide your staff with training and marketing suggestions.

Again, thank you for your kind manner.

Yours truly,
Your name

When you must be the one to say no to someone, you can choose to do it with respect. Often that means writing a letter acknowledging the other person's effort. As anyone in business will attest, one should never underestimate the potential positive effects of such a demonstration of good manners.

Here's a way to say, "No, I am not interested":

Dear Ms. Jones:

After several unsuccessful attempts to contact you by telephone, I thought it best to send you a note.

Thank you for your professional information regarding radio advertising for our company. Unfortunately, your fee schedule is not in line with our budget.

Please know that we at the XYZ Corporation recognize the importance of advertising. We will keep you in mind for future consideration.

Yours truly,
Your name

Saying Thank You for a Job Well Done

In addition to thanking the people who give you business, you should remember to thank those who've helped you perform the assignment well—subsidiary suppliers whose products were delivered on time and in perfect order, colleagues in other departments of the company who may have provided you with meaningful assistance.

Rather than making a thank-you call, use this opportunity to write a thank-you note. A phone call interrupts a busy person's day, and when you've said "good-bye", it's gone. A written note, on the other hand, is lasting.

It is tangible evidence of good work, that can be shown to one's boss, copied, and circulated to the entire department, placed in one's scrap book or portfolio, reread and enjoyed at one's leisure.

The note becomes a continual reminder of what a pleasure it is to do business with a person who cares.

Carbon Copy Etiquette

The use of computers, word processors, high-speed printers, and copying machines is causing subtle but visible changes in the etiquette of written office communication.

Historically, the carbon copy notation indicating the distribution of courtesy copies to other people was placed below the signature block, flush with the margin, starting with "cc," signifying "carbon copy." Now, with the invention of the high-quality instant copying machine and the high-speed printer, these courtesy copies are reproduced quickly and look like originals. We no longer receive carbon copies in the literal sense. Therefore, the new notation on the left side of the correspondence should read "c" or "Copy to," as in, "Copy to Ms. Jane Smith."

Each copy will still require a check mark adjacent to the name of the person receiving the courtesy copy. This is especially important when more than one person is to receive the copy.

CAVEAT: Only the original contains the actual signature in the signature block. All subsequent copies are to be left unsigned. The assistant who expects to make additional copies at a later date will make an extra unsigned file copy.

Business Card Etiquette

While the business card is a form of printed corporate communication, it is also an executive's personal calling card. It is the executive's responsibility to present the card appropriately and purposefully, keeping in mind that doing so adds one more favorable element in the perception of the total businessperson.

Here are some points to remember about using business cards:

Do affix your card to your presentation folder or corporate literature. Some people may not be familiar with you or the company you represent.

Do exchange your business card at a business or social gathering, but *only if* you are selective, and if it's done in private with the other person. If you hand out your card indiscriminately to everyone you've just met, you will likely appear childish or overly zealous.

If you wish to offer your card to someone you've just met, *do* have a conversation long enough for you to be sure you *want* the person to have your card.

Do keep your cards protected and fresh. They are the symbol of you and your corporation. Instead of presenting a shabby card, it's preferable to write your pertinent information on a plain piece of paper.

Do personalize your card, by underlining your name and writing a few words on the reverse side, if the occasion warrants. The card may then be inserted with some flowers or other small gift to someone who has been helpful to you.

Don't present your business card during a meal, whether formal or not.

Technology, in the form of computers, facsimile machines, modems and interactive laser disks, is changing the way an office operates, and redefining the ways business is conducted. In this mechanistic climate, it's very easy to forget that we are not the servants of the glistening new machines. Rather, the new machinery is supposedly helping us to do our jobs more easily, freeing us to do the tasks only human beings can accomplish. Personal communication between one executive and another becomes more important than ever.

CHAPTER SIX

CORPORATE GIFT-GIVING

Every company has two organizational structures: The formal one is written on the charts; the other is the everyday relationship of the men and women in the organization.
—HAROLD S. GENEEN, FORMER CHAIRMAN OF IT&T

G IFT-GIVING AND LETTER-WRITING ARE
   time-honored ways of expressing appreciation and
building goodwill throughout the world. While the traditional holiday season has become the main period of
gift-giving, it's essential to acknowledge the many special
occasions such as weddings, births, promotions, and even
the losses experienced by the people we work with
throughout the year.

People who attend our seminars invariably want to
know about the etiquette of gift-giving and written communication. Is it necessary or proper, they ask, for executives to recognize or take part in the personal celebrations
and/or misfortunes of their co-workers and clients?

THE ETIQUETTE OF GIFT-GIVING

A gift is a wonderful way to delight a dear friend. Frequently, half the fun of giving is choosing—the art of
finding the perfect thing becomes an additional aspect of
showing how much we care.

There's an art to business gift-giving, too, once we've
learned to ask ourselves some important questions:

Are we selecting gifts for clients, colleagues, or office
staff? If the gifts are for clients, do we have a personal
relationship with them? Do we present the boss with a
gift at holiday time or for his or her birthday?

Gifts for Clients

Yes, it is appropriate to give gifts to your personally close
business clients, provided, of course, that you avoid os-
tentation or any hint that your gift could be considered
a bribe.

The most successful business gifts are as individual as possible. Think about each recipient; never buy dozens of the same item to distribute to every client on your gift list.

Your choices will depend upon what you've learned about your client's travels, hobbies, and enthusiasms in the course of your relationship. For example, a fine book may be welcome—not because it's at the top of the bestseller list, but rather because it's on a subject the client knows a great deal about or has expressed much interest in, or is possibly written by a mutual friend. (And then you might try to purchase a personally autographed copy.) If you feel you don't know enough about a client to make an interesting choice, you might ask his or her secretary for a clue.

For clients with whom you are not personally close, you might choose from the gamut of less personal things, such as business card cases, barware, calendars, small electronic gadgets, and the like. Whenever possible choose a gift that is useful or practical. Gifts that advertise your company, products, or services may also be suitable.

CAVEAT: Any item bearing your company name or logo should be of fine quality and in excellent taste. Poorly made merchandise doesn't reflect well upon you or your organization. Nor do useless gadgets—just something else to dust—that appear to have been chosen expressly to serve as a background for your company's emblem.

Remember that your wrapping and your presentation—preferably in person—and your thoughtful handwritten message on your enclosure card are as important as your gift.

Foreign Gift Customs
The global marketplace requires knowledge of the customs of other lands. On the next page are gift guidelines for some of the countries Americans frequently do business with.

Special Occasions
Clients appreciate acknowledgment of the fact that they're "real people" too. When their children are confirmed, become engaged, when they marry, when the first grand-

Country	Hostess gifts, if invited to home	Business gifts
China	English language books, family photos wrap gifts in red paper	Logo gifts, magazine subscriptions
England	Flowers, *not* lilies, send to hostess the next day	Small, serious gift of fine quality
France	Flowers sent to hostess ahead of time, *not* red roses, or an even number	Small gift, no corporate logos
Italy	Flowers or wine, send to hostess the next day	Quality gifts, fine foods, Cognac, champagne, at conclusion of business
Japan*	Flowers, wine, or sweets	Status gifts, made in America or Europe
Korea*	Useful native gadgets, wrapped in red paper	Status French, Italian, U.S. accessories
Scandinavia	Flowers, *not* lilies	Not expected; quality leather goods
West Germany	Small hostess gift, flowers	American regional foods, art, logo calendars

*Invitations to meet the family or visit the home are rarely extended in business situations.

child is born, those are times they want the world to share their happiness!

If you're invited to celebrate with the family, it's fine to accept the invitation and send an appropriate gift. When the relationship doesn't merit such an invitation, you should nevertheless send a personal note of congratulation or good wishes.

In the event of disappointments or bad news, cheering words or tokens are especially welcome: do send flowers to the spouse of a business associate who may be in the hospital, do send a handwritten note, *not* a sympathy card, when there's a death in the family or the loss of a job.

By all means, send personal good luck wishes—a note or a clever gift—when a client decides to retire.

"Impulse" Gifts

An observant, imaginative executive will understand the value of acting on inspiration—sending flowers, a clever small gift, or a note simply "because." Why not send a token because the client has just opened a new branch office, or launched a new product and you want to wish the operation success, or because the client gave an inspiring speech, or has just received an honorary degree? Unexpected attention can make these kinds of occasions even more memorable.

Showing Gratitude to a Client

It is not always necessary to send a gift to a client we value. Here's an example of a handwritten seasonal greeting to a personal client:

Dear Joseph,

We never want to get so caught up in the frenetic pace of the holidays that we forget to thank someone whose business we have truly valued throughout the year.

May you have a peaceful and joyous holiday, Joseph, and may the New Year bring you much success!

Thank you again for your continued support.

Warm regards,
Linda and Wayne Phillips

Such a sincere, well-written personal note, regardless of purpose, will mean more to a client or colleague than a box of candy or a pencil holder.

Gifts for Colleagues and Staff

In most offices, colleagues and staff exchange gifts because they care about one another or because they want to show appreciation for a particularly fine effort on a specific job. Holiday and birthday gifts are also appropriate, as long as they are neither extravagant nor overly personal.

When members of the staff become engaged, get married, or become pregnant, the rest of the staff frequently arranges for a "shower" or surprise party. Executives are not necessarily expected to participate in or contribute to these affairs—that will depend upon the size of the company and normal office protocol.

In some large organizations, management may receive wedding invitations from everyone in the company who gets married. Frequently the policy is to decline invitations from everyone except those on their personal staff. It is not necessary to send gifts to everyone whose invitations you decline. However, a nice handwritten note wishing the happy couple a lovely life together is in order.

Generous Gestures

Colleagues' efforts or achievements deserve attention and applause. Why not send a handwritten note, a single flower, or a basket of fruit to the co-worker who completed a project *before* the deadline? Or opened the new branch office? Or landed a new account?

Before the book was bound and ready for shipping, the editor of a reference work on consumer affairs was surprised and delighted to discover a personal note from the publisher in his inter-office mail. The chief had read the galleys and been pleased that "this excellent piece of work is going out under our imprint."

When Help Is Needed

All of us endeavor to keep personal problems from affecting our work. But caring for a sick parent, dealing with divorce, personal loss, relocation—any of the strains of contemporary life—is difficult. The colleague who's carrying such a burden needs to know that there are friendly shoulders to lean on. A diplomatic note, perhaps offering an invitation to dinner, would be an invaluable gift.

From Employee to Employer

Under ordinary circumstances, one doesn't give presents to the boss or to one's superiors. There are two good reasons for this: the average employer could be embarrassed by receiving a gift that he or she would know was beyond an employee's means, or an employee's sincere gesture of appreciation or holiday goodwill might easily be misinterpreted as a bit of apple-polishing.

How, then, do you convey good wishes or gratitude to a superior? You might write an especially thoughtful letter, telling how much your association with the company has meant to you. Such a personal statement is often more meaningful and affecting than any gift you might buy.

A divisional manager told us how deeply touched he was to receive a special thank you from a member of his staff.

Dear Mr. Grant,

I wanted to send you a special holiday greeting—a "thank you" from the heart.

This was a rather tumultuous year for the company. There were many deadlines we didn't think we'd meet; there was the "Mother Lode" account we almost lost, but we did more than survive, we actually came out ahead!

Through those trying times your trust in me never wavered. I appreciated that vote of confidence then, and I recognize how much I've learned from you. Thank you for the freedom you've given me in implementing some new concepts, and thank you for valuing what I do.

May you have a wonderful holiday!

Yours sincerely,
Charles Korwin

In the case of a longstanding, close relationship, it would not be inappropriate to give a small, meaningful present to a superior. If, for example, the person was known to be a collector of, say, old sheet music, maps, or antique toy soldiers, adding a fine piece to the collection would be a superb, thoughtful gift.

Similarly, if you had developed the "tradition" of baking an assortment of holiday cookies each year, or framing the definitive photo of your department at the annual company boat ride, there is no reason not to continue in this lighthearted fashion.

Appropriate Choices

The honest affection and enthusiasm inherent in gift-giving may need to be tempered by the awareness that the people we do business with may come from other backgrounds or geographic areas, and be of different religions and cultures.

Think before you send Merry Christmas cards or presents to people who may not celebrate Christmas. Wishing them Happy Holidays will serve you better. It is not wise to send wine or liquor to someone whose religion forbids the use of alcohol or who may belong to Alcoholics Anonymous! And don't assume that everyone you talk to will attend midnight mass at Easter.

Failure to appreciate these differences might earn you a reputation for being narrow-minded and insensitive.

Cost Guidelines for Corporate Gift-Giving of Any Type

Many people consider the government income tax allowance of twenty-five dollars for business gifts ridiculously low in these inflationary times. But junior executives should be able to find a number of choices at that price level.

Upper management might prefer gifts costing as much as fifty dollars, and senior executives could conceivably go as high as one hundred dollars.

CAVEAT: Keep a record of what you gave to whom—for income tax purposes, certainly, but also to make certain that you don't give the same present the following

■ ■ ■

CUSTOMARY ANNIVERSARY GIFTS

There are other anniversaries to celebrate in addition to clients' or colleagues' wedding dates. Consider the anniversary of a client's long and profitable association with the company, the day a much-loved senior employee joined the firm, or the anniversary of an innovative department—such as the in-house public relations group.

Almost everyone seems to know that fifty years of service or wedded bliss is a golden anniversary. Here are the customary symbols for other years.

1st. Clocks, paper	13th. Textiles, furs
2nd. China	14th. Ivory, gold jewelry
3rd. Crystal, glass	15th. Crystal or quartz,
4th. Electrical	watches
appliances	16th. Silver hollow ware
5th. Silverware	17th. Furniture
6th. Wood, iron	18th. Porcelain
7th. Copper, bronze,	19th. Bronze
or brass	20th. Platinum
8th. Linen, lace	25th. Silver jubilee
9th. Leather	30th. Pearl or diamond
10th. Diamond jewelry,	35th. Jade or Coral
aluminum	40th. Ruby
11th. Fashion jewelry,	45th. Sapphire
steel	50th. Golden jubilee
12th. Colored gem-	55th. Emerald
stones, pearls	60th. Diamond jubilee

It is not necessary that companies adhere to these traditional suggestions, nor is it likely that a company will honor every year of service. In fact, most companies begin honoring employees after the completion of year five and continue every five years thereafter. An appropriate gift for a fifth-year anniversary might be a leather desk agenda or address book imprinted with the company logo.

■ ■ ■

year (unless the recipient was so delighted with your choice that "the same thing you gave last year" is practically a request).

Receiving Gifts

Gifts should be opened when they are presented. Saying thank you is always in order, but writing a note to say how much you enjoy and appreciate the selection is proper.

The Bereavement of a Colleague/Client

Unfortunately, death is an issue with which we all have to deal. How we do this will frequently set us apart in a most positive way. While many of us may feel awkward or uncomfortable in these circumstances, the importance of giving support to associates or clients during the period of bereavement cannot be overstated.

Simple words and acts may be of real help to the mourner:

If possible, speak to him or her, in person if that's possible, otherwise on the phone. It's not necessary to say more than "I'm sorry," and offer your presence.

Understand, too, that the person who has suffered the loss may remain silent—unable, or not wishing, to say anything. Be assured that your presence, your show of understanding is communicated. If the person does want to talk, all you need do is be a good listener.

Again, the most powerful way of expressing sympathy is to write a letter.

Dear Marilyn,

I returned from vacation only to hear your sad news.

My deepest sympathy to you over the loss of Howard.

Perhaps there is some consolation in the fact that you are surrounded by many of us who want to do whatever we can to ease your pain.

Warm thoughts are with you,
Name

When the one who is mourning is ready to return to work, do what you can to include him or her in activities and decisions. Acknowledge the loss, but don't dwell on it. *Show* that there is an active support system at hand.

CHAPTER SEVEN

ETIQUETTE ON THE ROAD

The business of America is business.
—Calvin Coolidge, 1925

A TRADE SHOW PRESENTS AN UNPARAL-
leled opportunity for the greatest number of potential clients to learn about a company's products or
services. As a company representative, you are also on
view, and your behavior, attitude, and manners may be
subject to as much scrutiny as your company's product
samples or corporate earnings statements. As we noted
in Chapter 4, an alert executive can create a positive first
impression—the *halo effect*—within the first thirty seconds of meeting a prospective customer.

However informal the arena, unless there's a special
company uniform or dress policy for everyone working
in the booth, men and women always wear corporate
business attire. The high level of excitement generated
at trade shows should not be confused with a party atmosphere. This is a work situation.

As at corporate group events, wear your *identification
badge* on your right lapel: as you extend your right hand
in greeting, it will be easy to read your name, your company name, and your title. If the name tags for the event
happen to be gum-backed or Velcro-backed labels (which
may damage fabrics, particularly those used in women's
clothing), purchase some of the readily available large
clear plastic pin-on badge holders, not just for yourself,
but *for your entire group*. This will preserve the unified
appearance of the team working at your booth.

PROPER BOOTHMANSHIP

Always stand whenever you are working in your exhibit
area. A seated executive may appear disinterested, in-

attentive or tired, and that's not the message you wish to convey.

Should you be assigned the responsibility of scheduling booth coverage, keep in mind that it's preferable to assign short shifts rather than long ones. Standing for longer than a three-hour period, even wearing the most comfortable shoes, is tiring, and not good for anyone's back or feet. Fatigue shows—in appearance and performance.

It's a good idea to do some simple investigation and learn where the information booth is, where the nearest exits are, where the rest rooms are, and where there's a water fountain, a snack bar, a moderately priced restaurant, and public transportation. Not only will your colleagues be grateful for this information, but trade-show attendees who stop to ask directions will appreciate your courtesy. Chances are you'll have the opportunity to make an acquaintance out of a stranger and to show that you are knowledgeable, helpful, and on the ball. The favorable impression you make will reflect on your company.

On the other hand, "I don't know" stops conversation dead.

Have an ample supply of business cards, pens that work, brochures, leaflets, or whatever corporate materials you intend to distribute.

It goes without saying that you know your products and your prices. You'll be expected to discuss them and answer questions.

Having identified a prospective customer, take the time to show how your product or service can fill that person's specific needs. To hand out a price catalog, saying only, "Here, take a look at what we've got and tell me what you want," will most likely give the impression that you are solely interested in being an order-taker rather than a creative problem-solver.

Handling More than One Client

When the traffic at your company's booth is heavy, you may have to deal with several clients at the same time. That's like being the only one in the office when all the telephones are ringing. And you can handle the problem in the same way.

Excuse yourself, for the moment, to Client #1, saying,

"Please excuse me for just a moment. Let me see if I can make an appointment with these other folks for another time, so that you and I can continue without being interrupted."

Then ask each waiting client whether he or she wishes information or is prepared to place an order. Give your packet (or handout materials) and your business card to those seeking information and try to set up an appointment for a mutually convenient time. Take the business card of everyone to whom you give your literature; jot down a brief clue on the back of the card to help you remember each person when you meet later, or when you follow up after the show.

If anyone waiting to see you is ready to place an order, estimate how long it'll be before you're free and ask if it's convenient for the customer to wait. Take the business cards of those who cannot wait, write yourself a clue on the back, and either set up a later appointment or promise to follow up immediately after the show.

Return to your first client, thank him or her for waiting so patiently, and continue with your business.

The Well-Planned Booth

A booth designed for client comfort will also be a pleasant place for the people working in it. For example, a thoughtful organization will make sure that pitchers of ice water and drinking cups are available throughout the long hours of the show. Clients may appreciate the convenience; the staff will need the refreshment.

A good number of small tables, with pairs of chairs (the straight-backed folding type, not big soft ones you collapse into), make it convenient for clients to talk privately with you; they also give you an opportunity to sit and rest, if only for a few moments, while attending to business.

You may be able to think of additional conveniences, suited to your particular type of business, that will enable you and your colleagues to minimize the physical strain of standing alert on duty at your company's booth.

The Trade-Show "Trap"

For people who work in any one industry for any length of time, trade shows can become like alumni reunions: one sees so many of the same faces year after year. In the highly charged, festive atmosphere of a trade show it can be enjoyable to reminisce—swap tales of trade shows past, of colorful personalities, outrageous adventures, and terrific deals that were made or bungled.

It may be a problem for a legitimate customer to interrupt such gaiety.

And if the customer happens to be a woman, getting the fellas' attention, even in these days of enlightenment, may be doubly difficult.

The particular woman in this story had just been transferred to the company's New York office and the trade show was her first chance to meet the people she'd be supervising. She stood at the booth for several minutes, while three men—one was to be her colleague, the others worked for competitors—stood in front of the display, talking loudly, laughing, jabbing one another's shoulders, slapping each other on the back. They were enjoying a great reunion. No one acknowledged her presence.

Admission badges at this particular show were color-coded. Hers indicated that she was a buyer/exhibitor, and gave her name and the name of her company. For four minutes she stood at the entry to the booth. No one spoke to her or glanced in her direction.

She moved in closer, trying to get into the line of vision of the executive whose company (her company, too) was sponsoring the booth. He turned his back and continued rapping with the guys.

She wandered about the booth, touching some of the handouts, looking at the display. Still, no one acknowledged her presence.

After about eight minutes, one of the young models employed to distribute the company's souvenir trinkets, returned to the booth. It was she who spoke to the woman. "I'm Julie. Can I help you?" And, noticing the woman's name tag, "Oh, does your husband work for the company, too?"

The woman answered, "I'm looking for Mr. Jones, Frank Jones. Is he here today, do you know?"

"Oh, yes. Mr. Jones is right there," said the young woman, and walked over to the laughing male trio.

The man she spoke to did not leave his chums, but called to the woman, "Yes, ma'am, what is it?"

The woman strode over to him and extended her hand.

"Mr. Jones, how do you do? I'm Harriet Nelson. I'm your new boss!"

After-Hours Etiquette

If the trade show takes place in your home city, everyone involved will probably treat show days as regular business days and head for home at the end of the day.

When out-of-town representatives attend a show, the home office may wish to extend its hospitality by arranging to entertain them, at least on the evening of the first day. In such cases, the entire group of visitors should be invited to whatever event is planned. Attendance, while courteous, is not mandatory (an executive may have relatives or friends to visit while in town); the invitation is.

Out-of-town visitors who are left to their own devices should make their own plans for the evening, or for any free time they might have.

If a contingent of visitors is in town and several members of the group do plan to meet, say, for dinner at a local high spot, or to attend any sports or theatrical events, good manners dictate that they invite all of their colleagues. The colleagues need not accept the invitation, but under no circumstances should anyone be allowed to feel left out of the group.

This courtesy is particularly important when there's only one person—a single male executive in a group of female department heads, or a lone female sharing the territory with an otherwise all-male staff—in a contingent that's composed entirely of the other sex. The group doesn't *have to* go out together, but the invitation should always be extended to each member of the group.

When there is such a group activity, an executive who doesn't have an early business engagement the next day would be smart to join the crowd. It's an opportunity to get to know one's colleagues better.

CONVENTION ETIQUETTE

These events differ from trade shows in that they are usually confined to members (and/or stockholders) of a single company, and the agenda includes a review of corporate performance in the period immediately past, introduction and explanation of new products or services, and the declaration of corporate goals for the coming year.

At a convention, all of your social, as well as your business, skills will be on display, including:

- meeting your counterparts from other branches;
- handling introductions—helping your colleagues get to know the people who work with you;
- hosting a business lunch, breakfast, or tea;
- entertaining colleagues—at a company party, a formal banquet, or a concert or play after the day's meetings;
- communicating effectively—giving a formal address or talking to superiors, colleagues, or subordinates.

To assure your personal success at such a meeting, you will, of course, have to do your homework:

If your group has an assignment, make certain that you understand what's expected, and that the necessary work is ready ahead of the deadline. If you delegate any of the responsibilities, be sure to give credit to all the people who participate.

Before the meeting, write down any questions or problems you or your colleagues have encountered and need guidance to solve. When you have specific information to gather, your questions will serve to advance the dialogue whenever you speak. Knowing how to get to the point means the difference between wasting valuable time with unnecessary comments and contributing to the sense of the meeting each time you ask for the floor.

Before the meeting find out as much as you can about any speakers, so that you can talk intelligently to them if you are introduced.

While it may be comfortable to stick with the folks you know from your home office, it's more appropriate to introduce yourself to new people. Circulate. Use meal times to get to know those people who, like yourself, have been asking good questions.

Take notes. Don't try to remember all the relevant information you hear at such a concentrated, high-powered event. You'll want a record of the people you might want to see again, the letters you want to write, the articles and books you should read. Remember to follow up on these intra-corporate leads.

BUSINESS TRAVEL

Taking the elevator to a meeting on another floor or jetting halfway around the world are both examples of business travel, for which there are appropriate ways to conduct oneself. While almost everyone flies nowadays, our advice also applies to trains, ships, or buses.

Elevator Etiquette

Young executives frequently seem unable to understand that there are others sharing the elevator car with them. We've seen groups of two, three, or more step into an elevator as soon as the doors open, stand at the front of the car with their arms folded, speaking at the same volume they would use in a sports arena.

When speaking in an elevator, or any public place, the voice level should be just above a whisper, only loud enough for the person you are speaking to to hear you. No one else in an elevator, bus, train, or plane, wants to hear your conversation, nor should you force them to listen to your private business.

Everyone in the front of a crowded elevator should step out of the car and to the side when the doors open, so that the people in the back of the car can exit. Always step briskly, because the people behind you may be in a hurry, even though you're not.

Traditionally, men stepped aside to let the women off first. While the rules are no longer so strict, the men should not stand like a row of linebackers, forcing the women to squeeze between them to leave the car. Chivalry may be out of fashion, but there's nothing wrong with showing consideration.

Escalator Etiquette

It may seem elementary to state that two or more executives should stand behind one another, and to the right side of the moving stairway, so that others who may be in more of a hurry can pass them on the left. However, every day we hear someone say, "Excuse me, may I get past you please," so it's conceivable that some people may be unaware of what we think of as a universally accepted rule. And, our own experience tells us that executives need to be reminded that conversations should be carried on in a whisper. It is not necessary for others to know anything about your business or social life.

Holding Doors

In today's office buildings, the person who arrives at the door first—man or woman—holds the door for the person or persons behind.

Young people, however, should defer to older, or senior executives. In fact, the younger person is expected to get to the door quickly in order to hold it for the others.

An executive who is host to outsiders is expected to open the doors for the guests and motion to them to walk ahead.

Whoever accompanies an elderly or handicapped person is expected to hold the door or give whatever assistance is necessary.

On the Street

Whenever he sees a phalanx of young executives coming toward him on Madison Avenue, or any of New York City's crowded thoroughfares, a retired CEO we've known for a long time plants himself in front of the group and shouts, "Why don't you get a parade permit!"

His point, though gruffly put, is well taken. In general, no more than two people should walk side by side on the street and, as on the highway, everyone should stay to the right.

Automobile Etiquette

When executives of unequal rank travel together, the junior executive is expected to handle all the details of the trip, authoritatively but not obsequiously—tipping the porters, checking into or out of hotels, arranging for the limousine or hailing taxis, paying the drivers, and so forth.

In a limousine, the junior executive takes the jump seat. A junior executive accompanying his superior and others in the boss's own car should ask where to sit.

Need we remind you that the speed limits are always to be observed? Getting a ticket for speeding is juvenile.

Taking Taxis

Do you know that in some cities taxis cannot be hailed on the street but must be telephoned to pick up passengers? Do you know that in some cities, such as Washington, D.C., strangers are permitted to share a cab, which will deliver each passenger to a different destination? Do you know that in some cities rides are metered; in others there is a flat fee per ride, and in other places drivers are allowed to charge per passenger?

Is it any wonder that people tend to fear being metaphorically "taken for a ride" by unscrupulous taxi drivers in strange places? A smart executive avoids this by doing some pretrip preparation:

Ask the executive you're visiting about local charges and also for clear directions, so that you can be authoritative when you tell the driver your destination. If you've no person to contact, get that information from the hotel where you'll be staying. Have a local map, so that you can see where you are and where you're going. Find out—from the staff at your hotel or from the person you're going to see—approximately how long it should take to arrive at your destination, and then allow more than enough time.

Carry small bills, so that your driver may easily give you the correct change. If you feel that a driver is dawdling in order to force you to pay a tip, simply ask for the amount of change you want.

Instead of Taxis

There's a sure way to avoid confrontations with taxi drivers, and to make certain that you arrive on time, without anxiety, knowing what the cost of your travel will be: hire a limousine to meet you and your party at the airport, take you to your hotel, and be available for your appointments.

All of these arrangements can be made by telephone from your home city. The limousine will wait for you, even though your plane may be delayed. (In smaller cities, where taxis don't run all night long, that's a definite advantage.)

In addition, you can charge this item to a credit card, thereby having a record of your local travel costs for your expense account.

Airplane Etiquette

Airports can bring out the worst in people. With our skies and planes so crowded, it's no longer possible to say exactly when a flight will depart.

Scheduling meetings to begin forty minutes after anyone's expected arrival time is foolish, and leads to the phenomenon we call Executive Stampede: the rude behavior of clock-watching executives who, garment bags held high, think nothing of mauling anyone who happens to be in their way in their maniacal determination to be the first passengers off the plane and at the head of the taxi line.

Spare yourself, your colleagues, and your clients the need to revise meeting schedules in order to cope with travel delays, by planning to arrive the *night before* a meeting. This will allow you to rest after a trip, schedule a productive breakfast meeting, and then use the entire day for meaningful work. You'll function more effectively and the people you do business with will appreciate your preparedness and punctuality.

To and from the Airport

If two or more colleagues are to travel together, it makes sense for those leaving from the office to share a limousine to the airport. Otherwise, everyone is responsible for getting to the airport on his or her own.

When the plane reaches its destination, colleagues should look after colleagues. Male and female executives all help one another with clothing, hand luggage, baggage, and so forth.

Female executives are advised to pack sparingly. One suitcase plus one carry-on piece is all each airline passenger is permitted. Everyone shares the burden of handling the materials necessary for a corporate presentation; your colleagues should not have to help carry your personal items.

Traveling Comfortably

As suggested earlier, engaging a limousine to travel to and from airports is a good idea, particularly when meetings demand that you also transport presentation or display materials. No matter how long it takes for the baggage to appear on the carousel, your driver will still be waiting to take you to your hotel.

Another option that will make your trip more comfortable is to await flights in the airline club lounge. These havens for busy travelers are secluded, comfortable places in which to relax until boarding time, and they're worth the cost of membership (even if your company doesn't choose to support that expense). Moreover, taking your colleagues to the club lounge as your guests will distinguish you as a generous person, and will certainly get your trip off to a pleasant start. It's frequently possible to reserve space at an airline club for a meeting when flight schedules get too tight for comfort, and just about all you can manage is flying into a city and zooming right out again a couple of hours later.

In Flight

Colleagues who aren't seated together but wish to talk may try to exchange seats with other passengers. If that is impossible, they may ask the stewardess if there's any space for them to sit together and talk. It's inconsiderate for one person to sit while the other stands in the aisle, blocking the passageway and interfering with the sight lines of people who wish to see the movie.

It's perfectly all right to chat with the person seated next to you *if that person indicates a willingness to talk*. However, you should be able to distinguish between a response that's meant to prolong the conversation and perfunctory politeness.

You, too, have a choice as to whether or not you care to listen to your neighbor's stories or immerse yourself in your own work or plans. To ignore a person who speaks to you is rude, but it is easy to send the signal that you are not eager for conversation: direct your attention to your own papers, the airline magazines, or lean back and try to nap.

Hotel Etiquette

If the company travel department has not handled your advance registration, executives should register separately at the hotel. Two male or two female executives who wish to share a larger double room may do so by registering together. Under no circumstances should a female executive register as the roommate of a male executive, even if they are brother and sister.

The visible intrusion of personal relationships into a business situation shows a real lack of consideration for your colleagues, who are forced to witness your behavior.

Business Meetings in Hotels

As a rule, one conducts business meetings in a business space. Hotels have suites, lounge areas, and conference rooms of all sizes for these purposes. Speak to the manager or concierge to reserve the space you and your colleagues will need.

In the event that it becomes absolutely necessary to use one's own room to entertain clients, here are some points for male and female executives to remember:

Always be sure to schedule *more than one person* for the same time period. When you have two guests in your room, see to it that they leave together; do not let one stay on after the other has departed. No one feels comfortable—the client or the host—when a single guest is entertained in a stranger's hotel room.

CAVEAT: The company whose executives repeatedly do business in their rooms may be perceived as stingy for not wanting to meet at a place where refreshments are served or service personnel are available, which would require possible additions to the expense account. The company may also be perceived as heedless of the safety of its employees. By requiring meetings to be held in the "bedroom" or hotel room, the reputation and well-being of a female executive may be compromised, and even the male executive may feel uncomfortable under such circumstances.

A female executive may invite a single guest to afternoon tea (see Chapter 3), or should plan to meet a guest in the lounge area. As a last resort (and assuming that appointments have already been scheduled for lunch and dinner), executives should endeavor to meet at the client's place of business.

How to Tip at Hotels

In the United States, where service charges are not added to the bill as they are overseas, it is customary to tip the hotel staff:

The *bellman*, who carries your luggage from the limousine to the registration desk and then to your room, receives no less than a dollar; three or four dollars for several bags.

This gratuity is paid also to the *porter*, who is sent by the bellman to carry your bags when you check out of the hotel.

The *chambermaid* receives two dollars per day, left as an accumulated tip, in an envelope marked "For the maid." At the end of a four-day stay, you would leave eight dollars.

If the maid is particularly helpful and fulfills special requests, such as hanging up one's clothing, she should be tipped separately for those tasks at the time.

The *concierge* is in charge of helping guests, and is not tipped for small services. However, if a concierge performs a special service, such as getting you tickets to a hit show or a dinner reservation at the newest four-star restaurant, tip him or her five dollars, or more if the task is especially difficult.

If the hotel's *travel agent* (or the concierge) manages to get you a seat on the only possible plane you can take in order to make your connection to Huntsville, Alabama, on a Thursday afternoon, tip as much as you would for a dinner reservation.

The hotel *doorman* who actively gets you a cab and offers a cheerful "Good morning" may deserve anywhere from one to five dollars—depending upon the weather and the number of guests waiting in the line.

The *bathroom attendants* are tipped fifty cents to a dollar.

The *attendant* at the parking garage gets one to two dollars.

Tip *barbers*, *hair stylists*, *masseurs*, and *manicurists* 15 to 20 percent of the cost of their services. (A salon owner usually is not tipped.) If you don't have the proper cash, you may write their tips on your bill, and charge the total to your room or to a credit card.

You are not required to tip the elevator operators, the social director, or the desk clerks.

It's so embarrassing to reach into one's pocket or purse and find only large bills when you want to give a small tip. There are two ways to handle this situation:

Ask if the doorman, or whoever it is you wish to tip, has change for your smallest bill. If it has been a busy day (and if everyone has been treated as well as you), he'll surely be able to accommodate you.

If you're hurrying to your next appointment, excuse yourself and say, "I'll see you later." An experienced hotel employee will know how to respond. But make sure you *do* take care of the person later, otherwise you'll be labeled phony and stingy.

Single Travelers

The great majority of executives enjoy traveling alone; they can get the most work accomplished in the shortest amount of time. However, the traveler who then must dine alone at the end of a busy day may face a difficult time. This is particularly true for women executives without male escorts.

Even though more than 40 percent of business travelers are now women, a sizable number of hotel and restaurant managers, concerned only with realizing the greatest income-per-table-per-seating, haven't learned that the female customer means business. It's no secret that a woman arriving alone at a less-than-full restaurant is often turned away with the words, "Sorry, we're all booked up." The restaurateur who "takes pity on a poor lady all alone" will likely seat her at the least desirable table—alongside the swinging door to the kitchen or near the rest rooms.

There are still parts of this country where men assume that a woman traveling alone is "available." Of course, this is sexual discrimination in its most blatant form. The woman executive should not attempt to educate, but simply maintain the most professional mien when traveling in this territory. Dress conservatively and carry a prop —such as an attaché case or a packet of papers—to indicate corporate status. If an uninvited stranger tries to get too friendly, ask the captain or the waiter to find the gentleman another table.

In her column in *The New Republic*, author Maggie Scarf tells of being "adopted" by a group of silverware salesman who recognized her predicament and came to her rescue.

While the situation may not be as dire for male executives dining alone, the possible solutions are the same:

You can choose to eat in the hotel. Within the past few years, hotels across the country have made a formidable effort to regain the reputations they enjoyed a generation ago, when hotel dining rooms offered some of the finest food in any town. With most hotel menus reflecting the contemporary interest in lighter, more flavorful dishes, dining in the hotel may be a treat instead of a compromise.

You can ask the concierge to recommend a fine restaurant and to make your reservation, securing a worthwhile table for you.

Or, you can abandon the idea of dining alone and see if you and a colleague can arrange to have dinner together. Or, this maybe a wonderful opportunity for you to relax and unwind and order room service.

Postcard Etiquette

When assignments take executives to glamorous vacation spots, it's often a problem to convince the "troops back home" that one is really hard at work. And yet there are times when you do want to remind the office staff of what you're accomplishing on your tour of duty.

Opt for postcards which the office can share. Select either pictures of the hotel, such as those found in the stationery packet in your desk drawer, or amusing cartoons usually on sale in the hotel gift shop.

Avoid gorgeous views of sunny beaches that will remind your frostbitten colleagues in Chicago of the lush life you must be enjoying.

In your written messages, try to touch briefly on relevant meetings or discussions.

Costly Souvenirs

The manager of one of the leading hotels of the world

shook her head in disbelief at the latest inventory shrink-age report. "Next week we're installing new hair dryers," she told us. "These are going to be attached to the wall. People have taken thousands—I mean it—thousands of hair dryers from this hotel. Dryers they know they can-not use at home, because we don't have the same voltage as the States. They think they're taking souvenirs. I call it stealing."

And, of course, she is correct.

Hotels provide assortments of toiletries and packets of stationery and pens, which guests are welcome to take home. Some welcome guests with generous baskets of fruit. Those are gifts.

But ashtrays, towels, bathmats, robes, blankets, ice buckets, and the range of furnishings a number of guests seem to consider take-home goodies, are the property of the hotel. They are not to be thought of as souvenirs.

Taking other people's property is rude, inappropriate behavior: stealing. The sad result of this souvenir grab-bing is that the costs of these items are added to every-one's bill—we pay more for hotel rooms.

At one of America's grand southern hotels they tell of a departing guest who scrutinized his bill, verifying every item and, pointing to a sixty-dollar charge, asked the desk clerk, "What's this?"

"Why that, sir, is for the blanket."

One of the hotel's trademarks was the heavily fringed wool plaid blanket draped at the foot of every chaise longue. This guest had stuffed the blanket from his room into his suitcase, unaware that management, in an effort to put an end to pilfering, had attached an unobtrusive sensitized label to every item in the guest rooms. During the long walk to the check-out desk, the sensitized tag on the blanket was sending an electronic message to the billing department. The guest was permitted to save face by purchasing the blanket he'd expected to add to his souvenir collection!

OVERSEAS TRAVEL

In the global marketplace, branch offices are scattered not only across the continent, but around the world. It's essential for American executives to appreciate that the rest of the world doesn't always behave the way we do. Our hearty handshake, informal "Glad-to-meetcha," and breezy habit of using first names almost as soon as we say hello frequently seem to the rest of the world like too much, too friendly, too soon.

Nor does the rest of the world behave in any one particular way. Customs may vary dramatically from one nation to the next. As always, careful and conservative behavior can protect against embarrassing, and often damaging, *faux pas*.

If you are to err, let it be on the side of formality. It is better, when overseas, to keep people at a courteous distance.

Some Hints Regarding Names

Never call people by their first names unless they have given you permission to do so. Americans get on a first-name basis as soon as possible. The rest of the world does not.

Also, the rest of the world frequently arranges names differently. For example, some Chinese use the family name first. Sun Yat-sen would be called Mr. Sun. In Spain and the Latin American nations, the last name is a combination of both the mother's and the father's family names, as Mario Vargas-Llosa.

To avoid problems, ask, "What would you like me to call you?"

Business Meetings

Appointments are a necessity when visiting executives in foreign countries. The casual phone call from your hotel, announcing that you've just arrived and would like to drop by, is unheard of. If there are people you must see, arrange to do so well in advance of your departure.

Arriving late for an appointment is interpreted as an indication that you are not serious about the business at hand. If you're not familiar with the city, rely upon the concierge at your hotel for directions and for an estimate of how long it will take to travel from your hotel to the meeting place.

Business Hours

The length of the business day will vary from one society to the next. For example, British businessmen rarely discuss business matters after business hours are over. The Japanese, on the other hand, consider a twenty-four-hour business day a priority. They will take a visitor to dinner, to late-night places, and continue the more or less informal ongoing meeting for as long as a visitor remains awake—and then be ready to meet the first thing the following morning.

Business Card Etiquette

Your business card is your calling card wherever you go. In certain foreign countries, it can be as necessary as your passport—and there is a ritual in its presentation. For example, business meetings in Japan do not officially begin until your business card has been handed to your colleagues. The presentation is quite formal: the card is held face up, extended with both hands, with the lettering facing the person who is receiving the card.

Upon your arrival in a foreign country, ask the concierge at your hotel to direct you to the nearest printer. On the reverse side of your card, have him print your name, address, and so forth, translated into the language of the country you're now visiting.

Many hotels offer this service. Ask the manager or concierge.

Foreign Foods and Dining Customs

Europeans commonly take their main meal at lunchtime, frequently relax with a siesta afterward, and then work quite late into the evening. Their evening meal is a light supper.

Americans tend to entertain visitors at posh restaurants, while Europeans consider it a greater gesture of hospitality to invite strangers to dine at their homes. Punctuality is essential, as is a small gift of flowers or candy for your hostess.

If you are invited to a "native dinner" where nothing is served that you have seen or heard of before, let alone tasted, be brave. After all, the entire population of this nation eats these dishes with no obvious ill effects, so why not give them a try? At least taste each dish. Not to do so may be insulting to your host.

In his book, *The Innocent Ambassadors*, the noted author Philip Wylie tells of visiting Japan during the 1950s and of his horror at having to eat raw fish! Nowadays, sashimi and sushi are popular foods, readily available across the United States. It may reassure you to remember that almost half the items currently on sale at our local supermarkets were not there twenty-five years ago, including: kiwi fruit, spaghetti squash, monkfish, and yogurt.

When in doubt: slice thin, chew slowly, swallow quickly.

It may help to consider that our favorite boiled lobster surely looks peculiar, if not downright threatening, to someone who's never seen a large, bright red crustacean on a plate.

You only have to *taste*.

Foreign Dress

One glance at the photos of people of other lands tells us that they dress quite differently than we do. However, one should not try to "do as the Romans do." Your clients and colleagues abroad expect you to wear the "uniform" of your office here in the States.

Women executives should bring with them an outfit suitable for social evenings at the home of the chief officer of the company. A long gown is not required, but certainly an attractive, elegant dress is.

Tipping Overseas

The majority of hotels and restaurants overseas add a certain percentage to the total bill as a service charge. Since not all establishments follow the practice, you must ask.

Service charges are supposed to cover service that is rendered. Nevertheless, you may tip extra if service has been excellent. And you should not be afraid to withhold a tip if service has been poor.

In the following charts, we show you how much to tip different employees in hotels and restaurants around the world. It's easy to see that customs vary widely, even in neighboring areas. If you're ever in doubt about what to tip, ask your host or business colleague about local customs.

EXECUTIVE GUIDE TO INTERNATIONAL
TIPPING WITHIN THE HOTEL
Per Day

	Room Maid	Concierge	Porter (per bag)	Doorman	Rm Svc
Austria	no	no	20–30 Sch	20–30 Sch	no
Belgium	no	no	50–100 Fr	100 Fr	no
Britain	50 p	no	50–75 p	30 p	10–15%
Denmark	no	no	posted	no	no
Finland	no	no	2–3 Mk	2–3 Mk	no
France	10 Fr	10 Fr	posted or 5–10 Fr	10 Fr	7–10 Fr

Country					
Germany	no	no	1 Dm	5 Dm	no
Greece	to 20 Dr	200 Dr	50–200 Dr	20 Dr	12–15%
Holland	no	no	2 fl	2 fl	no
Hong Kong	5 Hk$	no	2 Hk$	2 Hk$	10%
Ireland	50 p	no	50 p	50 p	no
Italy	1000–2000 L	1300–2000 L	500–700 L	500–1000 L	500
Japan	no	no	no	no	no
Norway	no	no	3 Kr	5 Kr	no
Portugal	5–10 Esc	100 Esc	50 Esc	20 Esc	5–10%
Singapore	2 S$	no	1 S$	1 S$	10%
Spain	50 Pts	100 Pts	150 Pts	50 Pts	50–100
Sweden	no	no	2–3 Kr	no	no
Switzerland	no	no	3 Fr	no	no

TIPPING OUTSIDE THE HOTEL

	Restaurants	Bar, Pub drinks	Taxi no bags	Barber, Salon	Cloak-room	Toilet attend't
Austria	included + opt'l 3–5%	10%	10%	10%	posted	posted
Belgium	included + optional small change	10%	included	included	posted	10 Fr
Britain	included or 10–15%	no	10–15%	15%	20 p	5 p
Denmark	included	5–15% to 5 Mk	included	no	posted 2–3 Mk	posted 1 Mk
Finland	included + optional small change		included	no		
France	included or 15–20%	15%	15%	15%	5 Fr	3–5 Fr
Germany	included + optional small change	no	to 5%	optional 5–10%	posted or 1 Dm	posted or 50 pf

Greece	included + small change on plate/busboy on table/waiter	20 Dr	20 Dr	20–30%	10–20 Dr	5–10 Dr
Holland	included	included	included	included	1–2 fl	to 1 fl
Hong Kong	included or 10–15%	10%	10%	15%	2 HK$	1 HK$
Ireland	included	no	to 10%	5–10%	50 p	10 p
Italy	included + optional 5–10%	15%	10%	15%	200–400 L	200 L
Japan	no	no	no	no	no	no
Norway	included	5%	10%	no	2 Kr	2 Kr
Portugal	included + optional to 5%	5–10 Esc	to 10%	15%	20 Esc	10 Esc
Singapore	included or 10–15%	10%	10%	15%	1 S$	50 c
Spain	included + optional to 5%	to 5%	10%	100–200 Pts	5 Pts	5 Pts
Sweden	included	10–15%	10%	15 Kr	2–3 Kr	1 Kr
Switzerland	included + optional change	included	included	posted or 15%	posted	no

You will notice that there is no tipping in Japan. That is because the Japanese believe that one should at all times do one's best work. To offer someone a tip for doing a job properly is therefore considered an insult.

It is not within the scope of this book to describe all overseas business scenarios. Many colleges and universities as well as private companies offer such training for business travel overseas.

A Guest's Etiquette

As discussed in Chapter 5, pleasant meetings are followed by a thank-you note. As a visitor from out of town or from abroad, you should acknowledge the hospitality shown you promptly. It is quite appropriate to send a note to your host the day after the occasion—even while you are still visiting the city.

Certainly, a note is essential as soon as you get back home.

ENTERTAINING VISITORS

You may be assigned to act as host when out-of-town representatives call at your office. Make your visitors feel welcome by being ready to greet them when they arrive. Be prepared with a choice of activities for the time they'll spend with you, rather than ask "What would you like to see now that you're here?"

Share with them your pleasure in your favorite restaurants, shops, and special out-of-the-way places. Create a packet of information about what to do in your town, include maps, local magazines, brochures, and so forth. Realize how lost people are without their local newspapers, and arrange to have their hometown paper delivered while they're visiting you.

Aware of how disconcerting it is to make your way around a strange city, arrange for transportation for them—a limo, or a car and driver.

Put yourself in the visitors' place, and treat them as specially as you would wish to be treated.

CHAPTER EIGHT

ETIQUETTE IN THE MODERN WORKPLACE

Make everything as simple as possible,
but not more so.
—ALBERT EINSTEIN

A S ELECTRONIC WIZARDRY EXPANDS THE volume of work we can accomplish and the new technology seems constantly to demand more and more, faster and faster, it becomes increasingly important to remember that human beings must not behave like machines. Good manners—courtesy and consideration— are a prime necessity if any office is to function with a minimum of anxiety or stress. A caring attitude should be evident even in those transactions which seem least important.

ETIQUETTE AMONG COLLEAGUES

Office-Machine Etiquette

In an office equipped with the most up-to-date time- and energy-saving machinery, there will nevertheless be times when there is not enough equipment to accommodate everyone's needs at once.

When there's a line of people waiting to use the copy machine, and you have dozens of pages to copy, allow the colleague who has only a few pages to copy to go ahead of you. A large assignment that will tie up the machine for a long time may prevent many people from finishing more immediate, smaller jobs. If a lengthy assignment can be interrupted, always try to accommodate someone who needs just a page or two.

After running off a sizable number of copies, check the paper supply. If the well is nearly empty, fill it with paper.

If the warning lights indicate that the machine wants toner, or Product X or Item Y, don't return to your desk and leave the job for the next person, do it yourself. Or summon the person in charge of maintaining the machine.

We all know that paper can jam in a copier. If that happens while you're using the machine, fix the trouble yourself, call the person in charge, or report the trouble to the office supervisor. Don't leave the problem for someone else to deal with.

We mention copy machines only because they're most recognizable to the greatest number of people. The same principles of courtesy and commonsense apply to the fax machine, the telex machine, and other equipment found in the modern office.

Facilities for Employees

In addition to maintaining an exclusive executive dining room, many companies give employees a chance to economize by providing an employees' kitchen. It's essential that everyone treat this area with respect.

Although this may appear painfully obvious, each time you use an appliance, such as the toaster, microwave, or oven, you are responsible for keeping it absolutely clean. Leftovers must either be thrown away or wrapped and stored immediately. Food odors not only attract pests, they permeate the office. Many people cannot work well when they're inhaling the aroma of onions or pizza.

If there's a company coffee urn, treat it like the copy machine paper well—if it's empty, fill it. As you sip the last cup of coffee in the carafe, start a new pot.

No matter how friendly everyone in your office happens to be, foods in a refrigerator or freezer should be clearly labeled. Whoever "borrows" another's sandwich or dessert should ask permission, and replace it as soon as possible.

Of course, companies devise their own ways of assigning kitchen responsibilities. What's important is that no one shirks kitchen duty on the grounds that "I did it last time, why doesn't somebody else do it today?"

Unisex Facilities

Where there's an employee lounge, rather than separate men's and women's rest rooms, gentlemen should put the seat down and close the lid after they've used a toilet, just as they do at home.

Respect for Colleagues' Space

Moveable mid-height partitions are undoubtedly more cost-efficient than permanent floor-to-ceiling walls. It's simpler to illuminate and air-condition an entire floor than separate offices. And partial walls are easy to rearrange when a new configuration becomes desirable. What partitions don't do is make it convenient for people with differing work habits to work in neighboring modules.

A client told us about an employee whose productivity slipped alarmingly shortly after the department's floor plan was changed. The employee began to arrive very early, take long lunch periods, and stay very late. Her work improved, but he was concerned about the long hours she put in on both sides of a rather empty day.

"I can't get my work done while Harry Jones is in his office," she explained. Harry Jones occupied the cubicle on the other side of her partition.

"For one thing, he smokes constantly. I don't know if I'm allergic to smoke or not, but I can't stand the smell of it and I start to cough.

"Then there's another thing. Guys are always coming in to shoot the breeze with him, and I can hear every word they say. When he's on the phone I hear all of his jokes. That's the way he does his job, fine. But the work I do demands concentration, and I can't concentrate when there's so much loud talk going on. I've tried to ask him to speak softly, but he laughs and says, 'Girlie, if you wanna be in the ball park you gotta play the game.' "

This woman had the misfortune of encountering an inconsiderate colleague who was also a sexist. In her case, it required intervention by a superior to remind the other employee that

- the large conference room (and most offices have one) is the proper place to entertain visitors or colleagues who feel the need to relax and chat.
- smoking pollutes the air in the office and is distressing to others. People who need to smoke should do so in places set aside for that purpose.
- conversations in open-plan offices, like conversations in elevators, should be carried on softly. No one else should have to listen to other people's business or private affairs.

• proper etiquette demands that a person working in an open-space office who entertains visitors, smokes, and uses the telephone to conduct a major part of his or her business have the courtesy to ask the neighboring colleague, "Does it bother you . . . ?"

Her superior reminded the young woman that when another person's habits make it impossible for you to do your work (or live your life), it is a false sense of good manners to permit yourself to be treated in such an inconsiderate manner. If stating your objections calmly and succinctly does no good, it may be that the next step is to go higher.

Personal Decor
Whether they're spacious four-windowed corner suites or tiny cubicles, offices inevitably reflect the personality of their occupants. Unless the executive is a famed collector or connoisseur of exotica, it's best to keep it simple.

To personalize a business space, it is appropriate to use photos, as well as diplomas, awards, and honors. Plants may lend a note of warmth, but they should not hang from the ceiling or require someone else's care while you are away on business or holiday. It's best to avoid framed mottoes, since you risk alienating clients and colleagues who do not share your opinions.

We sometimes read about personalities whose children or pets accompany them to the office. This is highly unusual and inappropriate.

Dropping In
Offices with open doors and even cubicles with no doors are private domains. When you frequently appear in the doorway of a colleague's office and ask "Are you busy?" you are interrupting his or her train of thought. You may mean well, but it's as inconsiderate as visiting friends when you haven't been invited.

Management consultants call this the Nomad Personality. They advise colleagues to interrupt visiting Nomads and ask them to do a favor they can't refuse—such as checking out a committee list or a source of statistics. This tactic is designed to remind the Nomad that his or her own work is waiting to be done.

EXECUTIVE BEHAVIOR IN THE WORKPLACE

Within every giant corporation there are numerous smaller entities. The way a young executive treats the people within her or his small sphere will affect the quality of work produced by that mini-organization.

Executives and Assistants

Today secretaries are usually referred to as assistants, or administrative assistants. The former designation, which suggested a poorly compensated, dead-end job, has been discarded in favor of a term that implies a greater level of professionalism and upward mobility.

Whether you have a personal assistant, or share one with colleagues, it's necessary that you and your assistant both have the same understanding of the work to be done, how you want it organized, and when it's due. "I thought you knew that," usually indicates that the task wasn't adequately explained. It's unrealistic to expect an assistant to ask all the right questions, or to know everything immediately.

As with any personal relationship, forging the executive-assistant affiliation is a process that takes time. Even the most willing or experienced partners do not immediately dance the same steps at the same tempo.

Courtesy, mutual respect, and a keen sense of balance are required. The alert assistant will know when you are under pressure, and lighten the burden by handling visitors or phone calls with tact. The courteous executive will be mindful of an aide's work load and outside responsibilities and not make continual demands which threaten to turn the assistant into the twentieth-century version of an indentured servant.

Being bossy never made anyone a boss. It merely made them unpopular.

Subsidiary Personnel

The folks who work in the mail room, or the supply department, or the numerous areas that support any company's operations, have different kinds of jobs. Period. It is just as important to show them the same courtesy and respect one shows members of the same department.

Any executive worth the title knows he or she can't run the company without them.

Setting Standards

It's the personnel department's job to make the organization's goals and ideals clear to each new hire. But as the executive, it is nevertheless your responsibility to see that your assistant conforms to your, and the company's, standards.

Human Resources may say that each employee is expected to use correct grammar. The employee may nod enthusiastically. Could one sensibly disagree? But it is you, the executive, who will discover, after a few conversations, that your assistant persists in saying "as of yet" when proper usage is "as yet"; or says "if I would have known" when proper usage is "if I had known," or "between you and I" instead of "between you and me," and so on.

You may realize after a time that your otherwise capable assistant tends to be thoughtless, or exercises poor judgment when talking to your clients or colleagues. Painful though it may be, you, as the executive, must speak to your assistant privately, and quietly, yet forcefully, make it clear that "This is something that is very important to me, and I think it should be important to you. . . ." Most assistants will gladly accept criticism as evidence of interest, particularly from a boss who has demonstrated fairness and is generous with praise when work is well done.

Of course, if, after repeated conferences, the assistant does not seem to change, it may be necessary to schedule a meeting at which the executive tells the assistant that he or she must seek a replacement, and explains the reasons for such a drastic action.

A good executive will offer positive suggestions rather than negative, destructive criticism. "Why don't we try it this way next time?" is infinitely more effective than "You should never have done such a stupid thing!"

The executive who knows what he or she wants, allows his people to use their own creativity in achieving periodic goals, and then gives ample credit when he gets what he asked for, will develop a loyal, dynamic, productive, winning team.

Referring to One's Assistant

Depending upon the degree of formality throughout the office, first names may be acceptable when boss and assistant are working together in private. When visitors are present, however, she or he is properly introduced as: "This is Ms. (or Mrs. or Mr.) Johnson, my assistant." If she (or he) is to remain in the office, possibly to take notes on the meeting, the executive should say, "I've asked her to stay and take notes on our meeting." Ms. Johnson should be introduced to the visitors whom she does not know.

When your assistant brings informational material into a meeting room where others are present, merely say, "Thank you, Mary (or Ms. Jones, according to company practice)." She may nod, respond, "You're welcome, Mrs. Brown," ask if you wish anything else, and leave the room.

Under no circumstances should a female assistant be referred to as "my girl." Would any executive refer to a male secretary as "my boy"? Use either the person's name ("I'll have Mrs. Swenson call you later with that information"), or position ("I'll have my assistant call you with that information").

Taking Your Assistant to Lunch

At our seminars, clients often ask whether it's all right to invite their assistants to lunch, especially assistants of the opposite sex. When we ask, "Why not?" they mumble about "office gossip and that sort of thing." Their worries are unfounded.

If you and your assistant need to plan the next day's meeting, or arrange for carrying on business while one of you will be on vacation, it's perfectly natural to get away from the office so that you can talk without interruptions. Power breakfasts and business lunches aren't expressly for wooing clients, after all.

And what about taking one's assistant to lunch because he just did a terrific job and made the whole department look good? Or because she and her husband are saving every penny for a down payment on a house, and she'd be delighted to skip her daily yogurt or tuna fish sandwich for a change?

The Coffee Controversy

As stated above, the assistant's responsibility is to take care of all matters concerning the office so that the executive can be free to do the job he or she is good at.

The executive shouldn't feel uncomfortable about asking the assistant to get lunch or to get coffee on company time. A capable assistant should therefore be ready to assist the executive she or he works for by making coffee—or getting it from the coffee wagon, the company urn, or the shop around the corner. If the boss wants to work at his or her desk, getting lunch is a small part of the day's job.

"Rush" Jobs

When an executive wants an assignment done "immediately, if not sooner," she has a right to expect her assistant, or member of the subordinate staff, to do the work as quickly as possible.

Doing the Boss's Shopping

Whether it's appropriate to ask an assistant to select gifts for spouses, children, or colleagues depends upon the quality of the relationship between the executive and the assistant. Executives who feel free to make such requests should not expect the assistant to forfeit a lunch hour to look for the perfect present. However long it takes to do this job should be "company" time.

The Children's Typing

The executive who asks an assistant to type his children's homework assignments is abusing the relationship. The assistant is no longer doing the boss's work, but the boss's child's work, and that child should be encouraged to take responsibility for his or her own obligations.

About Gossip

It's wonderful to be able to have a good, healthy laugh when something silly or unexpected happens to someone everyone knows in the office. "Mr. Halliwell's tie got caught in his attaché case and when he stood up the case was hanging from his neck!"

And if a member of the staff wins the lottery, that's

the sort of great event that deserves balloons and whistles—at least in the employee lounge.

But whispering about personal, private, or financial goings-on in the lives of colleagues is totally inappropriate. Executives never indulge in such conversations with assistants. Nor should assistants gossip about their bosses.

However, part of an assistant's job is to know what's going on, and if he (or she) learns some bit of *business* information that might be of interest to his boss, he should definitely pass it on. That's not spreading gossip, it's keeping the boss informed.

CONDUCTING BUSINESS

Either the executive or the assistant may serve as "host" and conduct a visitor from the reception area to the executive's office, reaching to open doors for the visitor. In the case of a revolving door, the host enters before the visitor to control the speed of the revolving door and to be ready to direct the client as soon as he or she exits.

If it's necessary to take an elevator, the host should hold the door for the visitor. As noted in Chapter 7, executives who block the entrance or talk loudly are indulging in inappropriate behavior. To a visitor, this may suggest an arrogant executive "family."

A Visitor's Guide to Appointments

As the one who is visiting an executive in his office, you should be on time, preferably a few minutes early.

Immediately identify yourself to the receptionist and tell him/her who you want to see. Present your business card so that the receptionist can "see" your name and your company's name before announcing you. When you've been announced, thank the receptionist.

If you have a coat, hang it in the closet, or fold it neatly and place it on your lap or on the banquette next to you in the waiting area.

Stand when you are approached by the person you've come to see or by his/her assistant.

After the meeting thank the receptionist as you leave.

Receiving Visitors

The way in which a visitor is welcomed can set the tone of the entire meeting. Gone are the days when executives played "power games" and tried to exert dominance by making outsiders feel as uncomfortable as possible.

We remember a brilliant CEO no more than five foot two inches tall whose office was furnished with furniture made expressly to fit his delicate proportions. Even the doorways were low. As most of the executives working with him happened to be quite tall, he seemed never more gleeful than when they were obviously off-balance—trying to avoid bumping their heads, or wondering where to put their long legs and how to keep from toppling over in his tiny chairs!

Today's executive always rises when a visiting client or senior executive enters his or her office. Upon being introduced, women executives rise also. Formerly, women were permitted to sit during an introduction.

The executive comes out from behind the desk and goes to shake hands with the visitor/client. By moving away from the symbolic "protection" of his (or her) desk he turns what might have been an adversarial relationship into one of compatibility. Let's sit and talk as equals, he implies, dragging a chair up to the sofa, or leading his visitor to the little round table in the conversation area.

Executives who smoke will have ashtrays handy for visitors who also smoke. Nonsmokers should, nonetheless, have clean ashtrays available in case clients wish to smoke. Nowadays, it's courteous to ask, "Do you mind if I smoke?"

Instruct your assistant to defer all calls. It's discourteous to a visitor to talk at length on the telephone in his or her presence. If you are expecting an important call, let your visitor know that, and, if conditions warrant, go to another area to take the call.

When the discussion is over, the host/executive stands, extends his or her hand, and says, "Thank you for coming," or "I'm glad we were able to have this talk," or "I'm sorry, I have another meeting scheduled."

Hugs and Kisses

In an overzealous attempt to appear "glad ta see ya," some executives are blurring the distinction between social and business etiquette. However affectionate and demonstrative you may be in private, shaking hands remains the only appropriate way of greeting people in business.

In the world of entertainment, business is habitually conducted on a much more emotional level. In this society, a kiss on the cheek has become the equivalent of a handshake; elsewhere, it's seen as phony behavior.

Bear hugs and loud hellos belong in the fraternity house and appear juvenile in a corporate setting. Old college chums who are glad to see one another may perhaps grab each other's arm with the left hand while shaking right hands warmly.

Of course, if a colleague or department has just won an award, showing emotion by hugging or kissing is a way of celebrating—and then, everybody goes back to business.

As we've said before, executive behavior starts at the top. A boss who is in the habit of kissing visitors on both cheeks or clasping them to his or her bosom when they arrive and when they leave can set the tone for subordinates and become known for an expansive management style. When the boss isn't there, everyone can be more formal.

Conducting Discussions

To have a fruitful discussion it's essential that each participant show respect to the other participants. Listen to each speaker without interrupting. Listen without shaking one's head in disagreement or making involuntary sounds that express your reactions.

Respond to what has been said before going on to your own points. Question, don't accuse or assume. Refrain from nervous gestures, such as swinging a foot, playing with paper clips, or doodling.

In a meeting between two or three people, it's appropriate to say, "I'd like to take notes so that I'm certain I know all the points you're making," even though you may feel that taking notes is accepted behavior.

Remember, it's a meeting, not a battle.

Describing Yourself

One of the least effective things an executive can do is announce what kind of person he or she is. "Now, I want you to know that I'm very practical," or "I want you to know that I'm a very easy person to get along with."

We will not know, or accept, the information merely because we've been told. We will know it when we see evidence of the fact. Demonstration, not description, is what convinces us.

Lingering Visitors

Sometimes visitors will want to stay longer than you wish. A smart executive, or assistant, will make certain the appointment ends at the proper time. Instruct your assistant to buzz you with a confidential message at a certain time; if the visitor stays on, your assistant buzzes again; the third time, your assistant enters, asks pardon for the interruption, and hands you a message.

This is your cue to read the message, rise, extend your hand, and say, "I'm sorry, I have to attend another meeting."

New Hire "Nerves"

Sometimes executives are called upon to deal directly with a client before they've had sufficient time to become totally familiar with the many details of the office procedure. Clients, interpreting hesitance as lack of ability, may get upset if they feel they're in the hands of an incompetent. After all, it's their time and money, and they appear to be wasting both.

It's perfectly all right to be a novice. But rather than trying to ignore or override your own lack of experience (like the actor who pretends not to notice that the door knob has fallen off in his hand), take the time to reassure the client by explaining, "I'm going to do this slowly so that we're both certain everything's correct," or "I want to check this with my superior. It will take a few minutes."

Disappearing Acts

Few things are more irksome to a client than stating his business to an executive or assistant who nods and then walks away, leaving the client alone at the desk for an unstated period of time.

There's surely a logical reason for the employee to go to another area, but the person left waiting must be informed. "I'm going to get the copies of our correspondence from the division manager's office. I'll be back in a few minutes," or words to that effect, will suffice.

Clients are busy people and their time is valuable. Don't assume that they will sit quietly while you go about your business, even if it is their business you are handling. Always tell the client how long a task will take.

CHAPTER NINE

SARTORIAL SAVVY

*You never get a second chance
to make a first impression.*
—Anonymous

I N CHAPTER 4, WE DESCRIBED THE *HALO* *effect*, the positive impression that comes across to us within the first thirty seconds of meeting someone. Rightly or wrongly, our decisions about an individual's ability and character are largely based upon our initial response to the person's appearance—appropriateness of dress, coupled with an engaging manner, firm handshake, and general air of vitality. We assume that anyone who can handle personal details so well will be equally meticulous in dealing with the demands of any job. We likewise infer that a slovenly person will do sloppy work.

Such snap judgments are not just a recently noted response to the ultra-fast pace of modern business life. Research indicates that higher salaries and faster promotions have traditionally gone to those who understand that appearance can enhance credibility. We may argue that competence should be all that matters, but potential geniuses who do not, or cannot, make a good first impression, consistently earn less money and advance at a slower pace.

There's no getting around it: packaging yourself is of vital importance. Job applicants who project the professional image effectively even command higher starting salaries—as much as 20 percent more—than those who do not.

WARDROBE BASICS

The components of the executive wardrobe have remained stable for decades. Brooks Brothers, one of the oldest and most respected men's stores, still carries a few of the classic styles it sold when the store opened more than one hundred fifty years ago.

As with all aspects of business behavior, every corporation has its own standard dress code. Top management usually sets the example, and the other executives follow.

Quality is the hallmark of the professional or corporate image. It is essential for both women and men to be seen always wearing clothes of excellent quality.

It's also expensive. There's no denying that good clothing costs a significant amount of money. But well-made, perfectly fitted suits of fine fabric are worth every dollar you spend because they last longer than cheaper clothes and never fail to look impressive.

Fabrics

Fabrics are either of natural or man-made fibers. The natural fibers are wool, cotton, silk, and linen. Everything else—Dacron, nylon, Orlon, and so forth—is man-made, or synthetic.

Natural fibers are preferred because they are generally the most comfortable. They "breathe," or absorb moisture, which makes them cool in hot weather and warm in cold. They hold their shape, yet they move with the body. And they signify quality.

Wool, arguably the most versatile of fabrics, comes in a variety of weights—from sheer wool crepe to heavy melton cloth; textures—from smooth flannels, luxurious cashmeres, and rough tweeds to nubby knits; and finishes—soft jerseys or medium worsteds to hard gabardines. It's strong, long-lasting, and resilient and can be worn almost year-round. Dry cleaning is recommended.

Cotton is also a strong, absorbent, comfortable fiber that can be woven into various weights and weaves, from sheer voile or gauze to oxford cloth, poplin, and heavy denim. Cotton can be dyed in an endless spectrum of colors. It's washable, but care must be taken to see that the fabric doesn't shrink.

Silk, while luxurious, is nonetheless a strong fiber with a very rich texture and feel. Heavy weight, or raw, silk can be used for suits. Lighter weights, such as crepe, satin, faille, chiffon, *peau de soie* or taffeta, are fine for dresses, blouses, scarves, and particularly for men's ties.

Linen is strong and durable, but wrinkles easily. Blended with man-made fibers it's excellent for summer outfits.

Man-made fibers are made of chemicals. They are washable and do not shrink or wrinkle. However, the fabrics tend to collect static electricity and retain odors. Because they're nonabsorbent, many people find them unpleasant to wear. They may convey an impression of less than first-rate quality. Ideally, synthetics are blended with natural fibers to add durability and make them easier to care for.

Fit

Few of us are a perfect size, able to take a jacket and slacks or skirt off the store hanger and wear them to the office with absolutely no alteration. Suits—for men and women—must fit without pulls or wrinkles: jackets at the collar, neck, shoulders, lapels, and sleeves; trousers or skirts are fitted at the waist, hips, and length. When purchasing a suit, it's essential to have the services of a professional tailor.

It's interesting to note that in fine men's stores, alterations are provided at no charge. Executives are advised to request the head tailor and to tip him (as one would a maître d') to ensure his diligent attention. Women executives who are able to find what they need in the ladies' department of men's stores can also benefit from this service.

The Value of Quality

Having recognized that purchasing business suits will represent a major expense, let's compare the costs of a bargain-priced suit and a classic and analyze their value over a period of time.

Suppose you find a bargain, a trendy suit that costs only one hundred dollars. It's not all that comfortable, but you can easily afford it. You also try on a classic suit of better fabric and with better tailoring. This one costs four hundred dollars. The difference in price is substantial.

You can probably only wear the bargain suit once a month since its style is rather distinctive and it's also a bit constricting. It's a ten-month suit, so you get ten wearings a year from it. You'd love to keep it for next year, but you notice that the lining is discolored and the sleeve edges look frayed. The style doesn't look quite right either.

Dividing the cost of the suit ($100) by the number of wearings (10) gives us a cost-per-wearing of $10.

With different accessories you're able to wear the four-hundred-dollar classic suit at least once a week. It's also a ten-month suit. That means you can wear it forty times the first year. However, because the style is classic and the fabric and tailoring are so fine, this suit lasts not one year but five! That's five times forty wearings, or two hundred times you can wear this expensive outfit.

Dividing the cost of the suit ($400) by the number of wearings (200) gives us a cost-per-wearing of $2!

The bargain purchase, then, is not always the item that costs less. It's the one from which we can obtain the most use. Applying this cost-per-wearing standard to other items of the business wardrobe, such as shoes, coat, or briefcase, may alter the way you perceive each purchase, and encourage you to opt for quality rather than settle for price.

The Corporate or the Professional Look?

Terms such as "the Power look" or "the Wall Street look" describe the most conservative manner of executive dress. It's favored by those in the banking, investment, and insurance industries. We call it "the Corporate look."

Only slightly less conservative is "the Professional look," appropriate for lawyers and executives of large corporations.

People in the arts, communications, or publishing don't follow these conventions. In those fields, employees are free to cultivate a more individual style. What works for one person will rarely be as effective for another, and will be scorned as imitation.

THE EXECUTIVE MAN'S WARDROBE

The business suit is the foundation of the corporate or professional wardrobe. Research confirms that the most authoritative colors—and the ones most flattering to everyone—are *dark blue* and *dark gray*. The suit may be solid-color flannel, gabardine, cheviot, or bird's-eye weave. It's the most sensible first purchase.

The *dark blue pinstripe* suit communicates the greatest

sense of authority. Considered the most formal daytime suit, it's the choice of executives who must attend a great many meetings. A *gray pinstripe* suit is almost equally as authoritative.

Subsequent purchases may be a lighter gray suit; a lightweight summer tan gabardine; and a very small, faint plaid (which has a gray to black tone). Unless the business is extremely conservative, a navy blue blazer and gray slacks will be useful.

Brown suits, jackets, or trousers are not appropriate for the executive wardrobe. With the exception of tuxedos, black suits are considered funereal.

Ideally, five suits will allow for plenty of variety in the executive's appearance while affording each outfit sufficient time to "breathe" between wearings. This will add to the life of the garments.

Style

In addition to choosing color and pattern, you'll have to decide on style. Jackets may be single or double breasted, loosely cut or slightly fitted, with more or less shoulder padding, a single center vent, two side vents, or none at all.

Single-breasted suits are uniformly flattering. Slim men also look well in double-breasted styles and in gently fitted jackets. Center or side vents are equally appropriate; a nonvent, or straight-back, jacket belongs only on a very slim torso. Padding should never give the impression that the hanger is still inside the jacket.

Perfect Fit

The fit of a suit is as important as the quality of the fabric and tailoring. When you're shopping for a suit, wear, or carry with you, the shoes, shirt, and belt you'll be wearing with the outfit. Explain to the tailor that you're very particular about your clothing and give him a tip for his extra pains.

When you try on the trousers, be sure to fill your pockets with the keys, handkerchiefs, or whatever you normally carry—they can affect the fit. Check the waist (slightly above your navel, and parallel to the ground all around), the seat, and the length of the crotch. Have the tailor pin wherever necessary: each change will affect the way the trousers hang. The trouser length is adjusted last. Have both legs measured—most of us have one hip that's a fraction higher, a leg that's longer. Cuffless pants provide a smooth, clean line especially good for the short man. Tall men, on the other hand, can use cuffs to cut their height. Cuffless pants should break slightly in front, and be about three-quarters of an inch longer in back. Cuffed pants hang absolutely straight in front.

If the suit jacket doesn't feel comfortable, you won't want to wear it. Are the armholes deep enough? Does the sleeve accommodate your cuff links? Starting at the top, check the collar fit. There should be no bulge at the back where collar and jacket meet. Lapels should lie flat. Make sure that the chest fits smoothly and the pockets don't sag or bulge. The bottom of the jacket should fall just about where your fingers curl when your hands are at your sides. Sleeves should end at the same place on both hands (about five inches from the tip of the thumb).

Remember that your jacket is buttoned whenever you stand, open when you are seated. Check the fit both ways.

Ask the tailor for a small swatch of the suit fabric. This will make it easier for you to select colors for the rest of your wardrobe.

The tailor will tell you when the suit will be ready for your second fitting. The alterations are now stitched with strong, temporary stitches. At this appointment you must make certain that every alteration marked at the first fitting has been made properly. If the fit is correct, the alterations will be stitched permanently.

Appropriate Shirts

The long-sleeved smooth white cotton broadcloth shirt is the favorite of the business world. Short sleeves are considered tacky. Straight collar and French cuffs, with simple gold cuff links, indicate the corporate look; straight collars and barrel cuffs are fine for the professional look. Button-down collars are acceptable on broadcloth shirts; on oxford cloth shirts they tend to appear casual.

All-cotton fabric may be hard to come by nowadays, unless one is having shirts made to order. Blends of 70 percent cotton and 30 percent synthetic yarn will be almost as comfortable.

There's an off-white, almost a cream or eggshell color, shirting that's barely discernible from pure white, which is especially flattering to men with sallow complexions. The tone has a wonderful brightening effect; it's worth hunting for.

The fit and style of a shirt are most noticeable at the collar. The collar may feel comfortable, but if it wrinkles, you're probably wearing a size too small; if it stands away from your neck, you've chosen a size that's too large. Make sure you have sufficient room at the waist and armholes. Shirt sleeves should extend slightly—no more than half an inch—beyond the sleeve of your jacket.

Monograms, if you wish them at all, should be small and simple, and are properly placed a couple of inches above the belt line on the left front. They don't belong on your cuff or at pocket height.

Traditionally, executives' shirts did not have pockets. Shirt pockets were designed to hold "tools"—pens, pencils, eyeglasses, and so on. For the true executive, these implements belong in other places—in the suit jacket pocket or briefcase, for example. By placing these things in the shirt pocket, the fit of the suit jacket is affected. (A subtle irony is that the most expensive shirts today are pocketed. However, if you can afford the shirt, you don't need the pocket to hold the "tools.")

Buy new shirts whenever you purchase a suit, taking your swatch of suiting fabric with you. Notice the effect of differing tones of white and weights of fabric. What you see may surprise you. Seemingly minor details become significant when you realize that you're not merely putting an outfit together, you're packaging yourself.

The Right Tie

Here, at last, is the chance for color-starved males to let loose and make some sort of personality statement that will be noticed and remembered. Well-chosen ties in stripes, dots, or other properly scaled patterns brighten an outfit and pull your entire look together.

Silk ties are by far the preferred choice. To some

they're the only choice. They're versatile, elegant, and correct any time of the year.

You'll need:

- solid colors—such as navy, maroon, or crimson. Never wear your navy tie with your navy suit: the colors will never match, and the one-color look is gauche.
- stripes—narrow, broad, or varied, they are always on the diagonal, as ties are cut on the bias. These are usually made of a heavy-corded silk *rep*.
- foulards—neat, small, repeated geometric prints. Foulard also describes the type of smooth silk fabric used in these ties.
- dots—polka dots, never larger than the head of a pencil eraser, may be regularly or randomly spaced. Pin dots are also attractive.

You should be careful about:

- paisleys—an all-over, multicolored, stylized leaf pattern which is of Indian origin. Finding the appropriately subdued color combination is not easy.
- prints—modern designs and color combinations can get very flamboyant. You run the risk of being known as "that fellow with the cerise tie." Unless you're very sure of your taste, save these for weekends.

You'd best avoid:

- club ties—pictures of yachts or organization membership emblems should be reserved for nonbusiness events, such as weekends on the yacht or at the club.
- school insignia—belong back at school.
- bow ties—they're either overly sassy or comedic.

The standard "four-in-hand" is the most appropriate knot to wear.

The Pocket Handkerchief
Despite the fact that they are frequently packaged together, the tie and the pocket handkerchief—or pocket square—should never match. Folded neatly and extending like a narrow line of color above the edge of the jacket

pocket, or tucked more freely into the pocket so that the points are displayed, the pocket square may be white or a solid color. Patterned pocket squares are usually silk in a small, discreet foulard or diminutive paisley. Either should coordinate with the tie and jacket.

The square never bursts from the pocket like a blooming flower.

Shoes

The corporate male wears a laced, plain-toe oxford. Wing-tipped laced brogues are acceptable for daytime use, but they're too bulky to wear at night.

Plain or tasseled loafers are fine for the professional look. However, they can project a note of casualness that may seem too playful for some clients or managers.

Black and cordovan are acceptable colors for daytime business wear; black is the only appropriate color at night.

Shoes are always highly polished, and worn-down heels are quickly replaced.

Suede, which Europeans consider fine for casual shoes, is not worn in any of these situations.

Hosiery

Socks should be long enough to cover the man's leg when his legs are crossed or when his trouser leg rides up. Elastic-reinforced tops have made garters a thing of the past; socks that begin to droop should be discarded (or added to your collection of dust rags). Black, brown, navy, or dark gray are all fine.

White socks are unacceptable except on the tennis court or golf course. Men who have found that they're allergic to the dyes in colored hose are advised to use thin white cotton or silk liner socks, and wear lightweight colored hose over those.

Belts and Buckles

The plain black leather belt will complement the navy or gray suits in your wardrobe. Choose one that's about an inch wide. Enhance it with a plain brass buckle.

Wide, saddle-leather "cowboy" belts and decorated, jeweled, or gimmicky buckles have no place in the office.

Jewelry and Small Leather Goods

A male executive wears a fine analog, not a digital, wristwatch and a wedding ring if he is married. As mentioned earlier, his cuff links are simple, plain gold. He also carries a pen and pencil of excellent quality in his inside jacket pocket.

Wearing class rings at the office is considered juvenile.

A slim, fine leather wallet, carried in the inside jacket pocket, is preferable to a money clip.

Coats and Hats

The tan waterproof raincoat is a necessity. Black or navy might seem more practical or conservative colors, but research has shown that these colors are associated with low-paying, blue-collar jobs.

The belted trench coat or loose single-breasted styles are equally acceptable. With heavy zip-out linings, they may also serve as topcoats in cool weather.

For a warm winter overcoat, choose navy or dark gray for minimum care, and consider cashmere or camel's hair for maximum warmth. Remember the cost-per-wearing theory when you buy—this investment should last for many years.

As research has shown that the body loses a great amount of heat if the head is uncovered, it is sensible as well as fashionable for men of all ages to wear hats. Choose a classic fine felt fedora in a dark, flattering tone, or opt for a warm tweed cap.

Ear flaps are acceptable only in sub-zero temperatures. Fur hats are a bit pretentious if the fur is real; tacky if it's not.

Scarves and Gloves

Dark wool mufflers, possibly cashmere with a silk lining, provide warmth and, incidentally, help to keep the neck of a dark wool coat clean.

Leather gloves, dark brown or black, complete the look. Knitted gloves tend to look childish.

The Man's Briefcase

An elegant, dark brown leather briefcase conveys stature. It can hold all of your important papers, as well as an extra shirt and even your lunch on busy days when you know you'll never have time to take a break. See that the corner stitching is reinforced, that the clasps are brass, and that the inner base is light, sturdy wood, not collapsible cardboard.

Not every executive requires a briefcase. For some, a large leather-bound pad is the ideal solution for their needs. Dark leather looks best and will provide the best wear.

The Complete Picture

Having acquired the elements of the corporate or professional wardrobe, the executive must also acquire the habit of noticing how he looks, not only when he leaves the house but throughout the business day.

Here are some things to remember: the jacket is buttoned when you're standing or walking. It's open when you're seated. Belt buckle and shirt placket should fall in a straight line. The point of the necktie should be in line with the midpoint of the belt buckle.

THE EXECUTIVE WOMAN'S WARDROBE

When large numbers of young women suddenly entered the work force at positions that had formerly been held almost exclusively by men, they were given stern advice on what to wear and how to behave. Told to be quiet and dress as much like their male counterparts as possible, they wore skirted suits of menswear fabrics, blouses with pointed or button-down collars buttoned up to the neck, and foulards fashioned into a stringlike bow.

Happily, everyone has relaxed a bit since then.

The latest research indicates that today's women executives understand the necessity for an authoritative professional image, but they also realize that *conservative* doesn't have to mean *drab*. In order to be perceived as skilled, competitive, responsible leaders, career women now dress for *credibility*. Or, as one young woman told us, "I dress for the position I aspire to."

The Corporate Look

Women executives agree that newcomers should always choose their role models within the organization. Notice what the most highly placed women consider acceptable attire at that corporation.

There is one universally acceptable look for the corporate woman—the matched skirted suit. Research has shown that gray, navy, and black work best as power colors.

The classic suit is single breasted, with a slightly fitted waistline and a straight or slightly flared skirt. Collars should fit snugly, lapels lie flat, and shoulders be padded enough for definition. Both jacket and skirt should be fully lined—lining helps the pieces keep their shape through many seasons of wearing.

Subsequent purchases should be wool suits in dark blue or medium to charcoal gray, and a small monotone plaid or check. With these, plus a selection of blouses, the woman executive has a wardrobe that can take her through the week in appropriate corporate style.

Women executives are now adding dresses to their business wardrobe. The classic long-sleeved wool coat dress, with its single or double row of buttons, projects a look of authority. The basic round-necked one-piece dress can be accessorized with jewelry or scarves.

Recognizing Quality

Fine tailoring calls for a hand-sewn lining, hand-stitched buttonholes at the waist and the sleeves, real bone or metal buttons, no plastic touches.

The well-made garment has ample seam allowances —one-half to five-eighths of an inch wide—with pinked or stitched edges to prevent seams from raveling. The ideal hem allowance is one and a half to two inches deep: the hem should be hand-sewn, with the edge of the hem faced with tailor's ribbon or lace.

Browse through the best stores, trying on—or at least looking closely at—the best designer outfits. Get acquainted with the look and feel of superior fabrics and workmanship.

The Color of Choice

Mainstay of the executive woman's wardrobe, and the best clothing investment she can make, is an exquisitely tailored black wool suit. A hard finished fabric such as virgin-wool gabardine, in a diagonal or herringbone weave, imparts dramatic luster to the simplest style. Wool flannel, crepe, or double-weight jersey are softer in finish and appearance.

Choose the fabric weight and finish most comfortable for you; consider the normal temperature of your office, and your rate of activity. You may be surprised at how lightweight and breathable good wool fabric can be. Your suit is wearable ten months of the year.

Black is authoritative, timelessly chic, and offers the most versatility because it can be worn with any color except navy, and look entirely different. A high-necked white or ivory silk blouse will project an authoritative look; a soft challis print will still be extremely professional, but less powerful. Switch to a silk jacquard top and the suit is appropriate for an elegant evening appointment.

The woman who falls in love with a bright red gabardine suit may certainly buy it, and even wear it to the office, at least once. Of course, if she wears it a week later, everyone in the place will notice "Uh, oh, she's wearing the red jacket again."

High color equals high visibility. Color always calls attention to itself. It's fine once a month or so, but shouldn't be relied upon as a staple in anyone's wardrobe. Your basic black, gray, or navy will always look right, and it doesn't matter how frequently you appear in them.

Identifying Good Fit

Unless you have an experienced local tailor whose work you know and trust implicitly, we suggest that you do your shopping at a large department store or in the women's department of an established men's shop where experienced tailors are on staff.

For try-on purposes always wear, or bring with you, the shoes, undergarments, and a blouse that you intend to wear with the outfit. It's the only way to guarantee proper fit. A long-sleeved blouse is a requirement with any suit. If the jacket sleeves are too tight, if you're not comfortable, you'll never wear that beautiful, expensive investment.

Jacket collar, shoulders, and lapels should drape smoothly. Shoulder padding should be in proportion to the wearer's height and weight. Armholes should be roomy enough to accommodate the sleeves of a blouse. Sleeves should stop at the wrist and should be measured separately.

Skirts must be roomy enough to sit in without pulling at the seams. Lengths may rise and fall in the world of fashion, but in corporate America they hover an inch or so below the knee.

Clothing Care

One of the advantages of a good wool suit is that it is so easy to maintain. Just hang it up on a wooden hanger after each wearing to let the wrinkles unfold. Dry clean a wool suit as infrequently as possible, since dry cleaning robs the wool of its natural oil. Yes, stains need attention: spot cleaning the moment the stain appears is best.

Blouses

The long-sleeved blouse is the woman's most versatile wardrobe accessory. There's no end to the flattering colors, patterns, and fabrics available. Necklines may be round, oval, V-shaped, with or without collars, or come with attractive scarves attached. Pleats, tucks, stitching, and buttons can add design interest. In your search for quality, examine the fabric texture and workmanship.

Always buy a blouse for a specific jacket, and try them on together to check the comfort, the colors, and the textures of the fabrics in combination.

CAVEAT: A washable slippery, synthetic satin blouse, while easier to care for than a pure silk which must be dry cleaned, will also tend to slide up and right out of your skirt waist. You'll be pulling it down twenty times a day, and wondering the rest of the time whether it's hanging out of your jacket.

Preserving Individuality

The woman who has never had trouble distinguishing one man in a navy blue pinstripe suit from any of the other similarly attired male executives around him, may still feel that she's sacrificing her individuality when she wears a suit. In reality, few outfits are more effective, or more indicative of personal style, than an appropriately accessorized suit.

Classic pearls add a note of elegance. Gold or silver chains can be smart. Lapel pins can be striking or elegant.

Earrings will lend authority to a professional look. Pearls with a gold rim are timeless, always in good taste. They should be in proportion to the size of the woman wearing them, and never larger than the size of a quarter. Dangles or hoops are inappropriate.

Small silk scarves provide a dash of color at the neck. They can be tied in many ways, and they make an expensive necklace or pin unnecessary.

Women may even borrow a menswear fashion idea and use a colorful pocket square in a pattern to accent a solid-color blouse.

Additional Accessories

Commonsense dictates that a woman may carry a fine leather *purse* as well as a *briefcase*. Size and shape will depend upon what works for her. The leather and workmanship should be the best affordable.

Carrying a handbag or briefcase imprinted with the logo of a fancy store or pricy designer may announce that you spend a great deal for your things, but it also suggests that following fashion may be more important to you than assessing true value or quality.

Shoes should be comfortable. Best is the closed-toe, medium-heel pump in black, navy, burgundy, dark brown, or taupe leather. Avoid pastels and suedes: they're much too casual for an executive look.

Hosiery should be a shade deeper than your natural skin tone. Matching the color of hosiery and skirt is effective for a personal social occasion, but much too trendy for the corporate look. Even in the heat of summer, the woman executive always wears stockings or pantyhose.

Silk-lined leather *gloves* complete the look in cool or wintry weather. Black, brown, Cognac, or burgundy are preferred shades.

Jewelry for women, as for men, is simple—a fine analog watch, a wedding ring, if she's married, worn with the engagement ring, if desired. No fancy rings. And use a fine gold or sterling pen and pencil.

The classic tan *raincoat* with a zip-out lining fits well over suits and is excellent for traveling. You may also have it in navy or black. For cold winters, choose a solid-color heavy wool coat.

Dressing for the Calendar

Most executives aren't involved in meetings every day, and don't take important clients to lunch every single afternoon. There are degrees of formality.

If you see that you have no appointments set for to-morrow, that your time will be devoted to planning an upcoming meeting, then wear the less authoritative clothes in your business wardrobe. Mix navy blazers and gray slacks if you have them.

Similarly, if a client has indicated by nonverbal signals that your "power" look gives her a feeling of inadequacy, have the grace, the sense, and the true executive ability to switch to something like a tweed jacket, open-necked print shirt, and gray skirt. Save the earrings and pearls for another day.

GROOMING BASICS

Information on the corporate look for men and women would not be complete without some notes on personal grooming.

Hair Care

Male executives are expected to keep their hair short. However, it should not appear newly trimmed. Regularly scheduled haircuts will eliminate the shock of the executive's shaggy-before and shorn-after appearance.

A woman's hair should always appear neat and combed off her shoulders, in an easy-to-manage style that flatters her face and doesn't call attention to itself. Long hair can be tied back or styled into a chignon. The woman's face, not her hair, should be the focus of attention at a meeting.

Skin Care

Cleansing, conditioning—or exfoliating—and moisturizing are the simple steps to maintaining a healthy complexion.

Many dermatologists consider exfoliating, which rids the skin of dead cells and impurities, the single most effective thing we can do to help our skin retain its clarity and tone.

A Touch of Makeup

Research shows conclusively that, contrary to what some may believe, a little makeup will enhance a woman's professional image. The goal is to wear makeup without looking *made up*.

If you're uncertain about which products to select and how to apply them, invest in a session with a makeup artist.

Wearing no makeup at all can make one appear austere, humorless, and lacking in confidence. That's a poor impression to make on clients or colleagues.

Nails

Men's fingernails should be filed short and round, kept clean, and buffed to a rosy shine. The use of clear nail polish is considered gauche.

The only acceptable nail colors for the aspiring corporate woman are clear or natural. Her nails should be just a bit longer than her fingers. Long, pointed, brightly painted "Dragon Lady" nails imply a frivolous-ness that's not welcome in the corporate community.

The woman who seeks a distinctive look may want to consider getting a French manicure. Here, the white portion of the nail is painted white, while the bed gets a natural polish. The effect is extremely attractive and professional.

Fragrance

A perfume can serve as your signature or echo your mood. When choosing a fragrance, don't just sniff the bottle, but rub a drop on your wrist and wait about ten minutes, until the elements can blend with your body chemistry. Every scent—and there are hundreds to choose from—will smell different on different people.

For the office, eau de toilette, less concentrated and less costly than perfume, is recommended for women. Men use cologne on their body and mildly scented aftershave on their face. Soap, deodorant, and talcum powder should be of the same scent or be fragrance-free, otherwise the mixture of scents will fight each other and destroy any effect you wish to create.

Women as well as men are advised to use scent sparingly. Colleagues should be pleasantly aware of it, but the aroma shouldn't linger after the wearer has left the room. Too much of even the most exquisite fragrance becomes an assault which, in the extreme, may cause sneezing or trigger allergic reactions among co-workers.

Citrus-y or light, flowery scents are more appropriate for the office (particularly in the warm weather) than the heavier, musky, so-called romantic blends.

CHAPTER TEN

CORPORATE COLLEAGUES

Work is not really new for women; what is new for women is the chance to be leaders.
—CLAY FELKER

WOMEN ARE AN INCREASINGLY VISIBLE and influential part of the corporate world. What with recent graduates entering the work force, older women returning to work, and the original wave of female executive pioneers celebrating ten or more years on the job, the board room is no longer exclusively a gentlemen's domain.

More than 30 percent of managers, 16 percent of lawyers, and 20 percent of doctors are women. Of the nation's executive accountants, 40 percent are now women; twenty years ago there wasn't one. In 1980, only 35 percent of the female officers of the Fortune and Service 500 were at the vice-presidential level, or above. Today, the number has risen to more than 83 percent. Women own 28 percent of the nation's small businesses—up from 7 percent in 1977—and are projected to own 50 percent by the year 2000.

They earned 33 percent of the MBA degrees and 14 percent of the engineering degrees awarded in 1986. Twenty years earlier they comprised a mere 2 percent of graduates.

Imagine the cumulative effect of these massive changes.

THE OLD CHIVALRY

Since the time of the Industrial Revolution, masculine gallantry toward women has been based upon the idea that women, being helpless, needed protection. Men automatically performed certain tasks for women simply because women were women, or rather, ladies.

A chivalrous man would open all doors for a lady,

order her meals in a restaurant, pull out her chair, serve her before himself, help her with her coat, carry her small packages, hail taxis, and walk on the outside of the street to keep her from getting splashed. During the eighteenth and nineteenth centuries, the gentleman walked on the outside to keep her from being struck by falling garbage thrown from an upstairs window. Being the one in business, the man also paid for the lady's meals, coat, for whatever was wrapped inside her small packages, and for the taxis.

The obverse of this code of chivalrous behavior was that women were automatically precluded from performing certain tasks simply because they were women. Mostly, women were denied access to opportunities to become successful at whatever careers they wished, careers that were freely pursued by men simply because they were men.

Having at last earned the right to compete for the positions they aspire to, women consider it an anachronism to continue to be treated like helpless damsels who would be in major distress were it not for the courtly fellow holding the door, pulling out the chair, or hailing the taxi. Women executives expect to be treated in a manner befitting their status, not their sex.

AN ATMOSPHERE OF COLLEAGUESHIP

Although *colleagueship* may be a clumsy, awkward-sounding word, today's women executives nevertheless feel that the term aptly conveys the appropriate sense of fraternalism, mutuality of endeavor, and concern. It also implies respect for seniority of position regardless of age or gender, for achievement and ability as well as for length of service.

Colleagues help each other to deal with doors, chairs, packages, coats, and taxis. Whoever reaches the door, opens it for the others; the person whose hands are free assists the colleague struggling to put on a coat while hanging onto a briefcase and a presentation folder.

The manners of colleagueship dictate that both male and female executive should rise, step forward, and extend their hands to greet visitors. Female executive hosts will pay for a male client's meals (see Chapter 2), and if the client indicates that he feels it his obligation to pick up the check, she explains that he is the guest of the corporation and the corporation is pleased to pay for his meal.

A female senior executive precedes the colleagues beneath her in rank, unless she is host of the event, in which case she ushers her guests to their places ahead of herself.

Stereotypical Thinking

Attitudes they're unaware of sometimes make it difficult for male executives to accept women as colleagues. Some men will say, as if it were an old saw, that a good-looking woman will never be serious about her work. Others will declare that a woman who's plain-looking is sure to be "mad at the whole world" and difficult to work with. They warn that a woman with children will pay more attention to them than to her work.

There are men who find it difficult to be businesslike with female managers. Compliments on one's clothes, such as "I like you in that blouse," are patronizing, as is the use of "honey," "dear," "baby," or "sweetie." These men would not address a male colleague as "boy" or "fella." Nor would they accept those nicknames from a woman executive.

Men, some of whom have been known to have temper tantrums and behave outrageously when they're upset or faced with an unexpectedly calamitous business situation, will dismiss a woman's legitimate anger at a colleague's gaffe with "It's the wrong time of the month."

When a woman presents a clever solution, they'll give her the ultimate accolade, "That's thinking like a man!" and call her an uppity female if she says, "I thought I was thinking like an executive."

. . . And How to Handle It

Dealing with such examples of the double standard happens to be a matter of etiquette. To transform her male co-workers into colleagues, the woman executive must first try to raise the level of mutual respect and politeness. Shaking hands and addressing one another by name is a way to begin. She can politely tell the man who calls every woman "dear" that she doesn't care to be patronized, and ask him to use her name. And she can request that the men in the office speak respectfully about other women. Eliminating the use of the pejorative is essential to effect a change in attitudes.

The late Golda Meir said that to be successful, a woman had to "be better at her job than a man." The first women to join the executive ranks of any organization will, for the time being, need to be, like Caesar's wife, above reproach—or, in business terms, exemplary executives. That women in business are still judged differently from their male counterparts is regrettable, but it's still a fact of business life in many parts of the country. The female executive gains credibility when she:

- consistently arrives on time, is thoroughly prepared, and unfailingly meets her deadlines.
- is equally polite, accessible, and compassionate with subordinates as well as superiors.
- judges work honestly, criticizes fairly, and contributes encouragement and helpful suggestions when they're needed.
- gives credit aloud to every member of her team who has been of assistance on a project.
- accepts credit and blame with equal grace.
- demonstrates that, serious as she is about the work at hand, she has a ready sense of humor and can laugh at herself or at a good joke.
- refuses to use profanity to gain acceptance from her male colleagues.
- doesn't try to preserve her place as the "House Female" but makes an effort to help other women gain entry or advancement.
- doesn't try to circumvent the office protocol or manipulate male executives on her drive to the top.
- keeps her personal and professional life separate.

We know of a woman consultant for a major software company who discovered that wearing her MIT class ring was the only way to prove her credibility at the male-staffed offices she visited. "I used to call it my magic ring and would sooner be late to an appointment than go to one without having it on." Of course, given the chance to demonstrate her product knowledge and problem-solving ability, she earned the respect of the men and women she met on the job.

Nontraditional Executive-Assistant Duos

The changing population of the workplace has altered the age-old male executive–female assistant combination. Good manners are essential for harmonious working relationships.

The young female executive and young male assistant. In this role reversal, executive and assistant are contemporaries. It is likely that they share the same frame of reference and are not burdened by the stereotypical attitudes described above. The female executive has the responsibility to maintain the businesslike climate of the relationship. That doesn't mean being formal, just professional.

The young executive with an older male assistant. An increasing number of experienced male executives, their jobs eliminated by corporate mergers or acquisitions, have had to accept lesser positions as the nature of their industries has changed. It must be extremely difficult for them to work under executives the age of their children, who're just learning tricks of the trade that these men may well have invented. On the other hand, the young executive may be uneasy giving instructions to an assistant old enough to be the executive's parent, when both colleagues know that the assistant could "do this job with [his] eyes closed."

If both members of this team can manage to concentrate on the opportunity to forge an energetic mentor-protégée relationship, if the older assistant can submerge his damaged ego and be content to assist rather than advise, the arrangement may work out.

Young executive–older female assistant. For the most part, older women assistants are former office workers who left their jobs to raise families. Now that the kids are grown, they're streaming back to the office—which bears little resemblance to the place they worked in twenty years ago.

Women who gave up dead-end positions beyond which no female had ever advanced, or who couldn't juggle the demands of job and family, may resent working for a young female executive basking in benefits that appear to have been handed her. An older woman may even expect her female boss to help her join the executive brigade, and achieve the success denied years ago. Or, she may sharpen her old skills and be a superb assistant.

A male superior may discover his mature assistant wants to mother rather than assist him. It's up to the executive to set the tone of the relationship.

Younger executives of either sex may be pleased to have an older woman as a confidante and buffer. It's well-known that a mature assistant will gladly handle lots of details and be able to maintain order in the most chaotic scene. The executives may also realize that the older woman's savvy—office equipment may change, but office politics don't—can be invaluable.

Older executives–young assistants. Enlightened executives usually seek the opportunity to establish a relationship with a younger person whose career they can guide. This *mentoring*—the interaction between a respected senior professional and a talented subordinate over a sustained period of time—seems to epitomize the mutuality of respect and concern that colleagues share. It is also the way a company style is passed along to the next generation of managers.

When men were the sole inhabitants of the workplace, a senior took a younger man under his wing. Today, women assistants can benefit from the experience. Also, the first women executives now have the chance to serve as mentors of young women or men.

Ground Rules

All of these relationships depend upon both colleagues' understanding of the expected behavior. It's the executive's responsibility to make his or her wishes clear. If the attentions of a father figure, a confidante, or a mother hen are too smothering, the executive should not become brusque, sulk, or withdraw, but should state his or her objections and request changes. If the assistant cannot make these adjustments, both may have to seek new partners.

An assistant who believes that his or her abilities could be used to better advantage by the executive should attempt to discuss those ideas with the boss.

The executive who senses that his or her assistant is about to make a play for his or her job may need to have a talk with the assistant to clear the air before their cordial relationship turns hostile.

Performance Reviews

Periodic evaluations of team performance are standard management practice. By giving each employee on the team a realistic appraisal that rates work accomplished and attempted, as well as work still undone, and allows each employee the opportunity to discuss the report, a young executive can gain every member's confidence and cooperation.

This is a management skill every executive should learn. Yet, a high percentage of employees report that they cannot get managers to answer questions or make suggestions. They complain that although top executives say "we're one big family," there's very little evidence of family feeling emanating from corporate headquarters.

Delivering Bad News

"Let's have lunch," is not the thing to say to someone you're about to dismiss.

Research has shown that many executives make this mistake. They seem to think that jovial surroundings will temper the awkwardness of the message they must impart. As anyone who has ever suffered this experience can testify, being in a public place only increases the burden on the already miserable employee who wants to scream but instead must swallow an oyster, suavely.

The compassionate superior calls the employee and asks to meet later in the day in the small conference room. Both deserve privacy for this emotional scene. The superior, painful though this task is, should not delegate it to a subordinate. Nor is it permissible to drop the bomb and dash immediately to another meeting.

The employee must have at least the semblance of a chance to question the decision (the executive must have relevant facts at hand), discuss severance arrangements, and ask for, and receive, help in finding a new job. Unless the employee has been guilty of an act punishable by dismissal, he or she deserves sympathy, respect, and as much help as colleagues can give.

Receiving Bad News

The best thing to do is get busy. Call everyone you know, set up interviews, send résumés, track down every possible lead.

Do not complain about what a miserable thing those miserable people who run this miserable company have done to innocent you. It's a waste of time—you won't change the outcome. It's a waste of energy—negative talk drains your confidence and resolve. And, it only makes the people who still have their jobs uncomfortable to be with you.

Let your courage, professionalism, and your supremely classy behavior become office legend, so that you'll be remembered long after you've moved to a much better position!

ROMANCE ON THE JOB

It would be hypocritical to insist that the workplace, where scores of attractive, intelligent, successful, energetic, and ambitious men and women work in close contact all day long, five days a week, twelve months of the year, is not an ideal environment in which friendships may blossom into closer, more personal relationships.

What we can insist on, however, is that people who do become involved in romantic relationships exercise judgment and restraint.

Advice to Employees

Understand that sex doesn't belong in the office. Proceed from there if you must. Keep your private affair private. If a colleague has the poor taste to ask if you and so-and-so are involved, deny it.

Nodding or smiling smugly to those queries will give the rest of the staff something sensational to talk about at lunch—and at coffee breaks, cocktails, the company picnic, the lounge, during inter-office calls, and so on. Becoming the subject of office gossip diverts attention from the quality of your work, which is all that the corporation is interested in. Gossip about your private life trivializes your value to the company. When the gossip reaches the boardroom, one of you may be asked to pack your things.

If the grand passion subsides, don't mention it to your co-workers. You'll be glad no one ever knew about the affair. No explanations will be necessary. There'll be no sympathetic glances, and no whispers about what could have gone wrong.

A More Serious Relationship

We assume that colleagues who become lovers are both single. If they work in the same department they should attempt to get separate assignments. Most likely such a request will be viewed as ambition. No one will pay much attention to two people who are *not* working together, whereas everyone will notice two people who don't seem to be able to get much corporate work done when they *are* supposedly working together.

Little by little, colleagues who are lovers may try to spend more time together on business trips, or the like. The relationship will gradually consume them. It may seem hardhearted, but the corporation is only interested in the work they accomplish for the salary they receive.

Many corporations don't employ husbands and wives. However, beyond making the company policy known to their employees, the corporation rarely insists that one or the other of the couple leave if they get married while working there. If they do, it's generally assumed that the executive with the better position and/or more seniority will stay on. If you and your lover decide to marry, which of you is willing to move to another company?

Interested Friends

Delicious though the idea of acting as privileged confidante may be, this is a temptation you must resist. Even when asked, don't give advice, don't get involved, and don't whisper to mutual friends. When the happy couple names the day, you can plan the party.

Advice to Employers

You may be an award-winning mentor, but this is not your field of expertise.

Attend the wedding, if invited, but do not permit yourself to be drawn into the whirlpool of employees' romance. It's flattering to be asked to give advice, but involving oneself in the personal lives of employees will make it difficult for you to then demand that they fulfill their professional obligations to the company and to clients.

Boys and Girls Together

Every office has them—flirts, kidders, touchers, huggers. There are the men who stare at a woman, sort of sadly, then shake their head and say, "Boy, I could go for you, if only . . ." And there are women who say the same thing to men! Women who lean against a man when they're hunting for a piece of paper on his desk—and men who do the same thing to women. There are men who tell off-color stories—and women who go into the minute details of their most recent massage.

These assorted talkers, lookers, and leaners are injecting sexual innuendo into the office, where it really doesn't belong. If you find yourself in an encounter with one of these types, it's up to you to stop that person's advances. A brisk, "I'm not interested," should do it. You can always return to your desk and get back to work.

Party Time

Corporate events such as the annual picnic and the holiday party are occasions when protocol is relaxed. It's easy for colleagues who've only caught glimpses of one another to take the time for a closer look, and to decide whether they like what they see.

Individuals who don't wish to get involved in extracurricular activities should be wise enough to have a drink, wait until the boss leaves, and then head home.

Women who are eager to discard the business wardrobe should remember that low-cut cocktail dresses or body-baring bikinis are overly revealing, and not appropriate for what remains, a business gathering.

How Sexual Harassment Affects the Workplace

Sexual harrassment is a form of sexual discrimination, which is prohibited by federal law—the Civil Rights Act of 1964. In the workplace, it is a potential time bomb. And it is pervasive. In a recent survey, more than 45 percent of New England management firms admitted that their companies had dealt with sexual harassment in the past year.

Sexual harassment is defined as "unwelcome sexual advances, requests for sexual favors and other verbal or physical conduct of a sexual nature . . . where submission to such conduct is explicitly or implicitly . . . condition of individual's employment . . . used as a basis for employment decisions . . . interferes with work performance or creates an intimidating working environment."

Harassment can take many forms:

Colleagues who have been dating for several months decide to end the relationship. The man, still in love, calls the woman frequently and stops at her desk to invite her out. She has made it clear that she no longer wishes to see him and has asked him to leave her alone. He continues to visit her at her desk. . . .

When a client complains to a manager that he's not getting enough attention from a female sales rep, the woman reveals to her boss that the client, her largest account, has made sexual advances toward her. She feels she can no longer handle the account. . . .

An attorney who refuses his boss's advances, learns that his annual review is significantly lower than those for previous years. The attorney who asked him out is on the review panel. . . .

These workers have suffered unwelcome advances that have affected their performance, and their livelihood, and which have created a hostile work environment. *Sexual harassment is very bad business!*

The employee who has been subjected to harassment tactics is always advised to report the incident to the personnel department, or to the designated social services staff. It's as important to alert management to this sort of incident as it is to get help in dealing with the trauma.

EXECUTIVE CHOICES

Humor in the Workplace

Nowadays, the ultimate power tool may be the ability to crack a few jokes on the job.

Corporations are sending employees to "Humor Seminars" that may not teach them how to deliver one-liners with the panache of a Robin Williams, but which do offer techniques on "how to dissolve tension and diffuse conflict."

According to psychologists, the sudden corporate interest in humor is a sign of the times. Rampant corporate restructurings, take-overs, and mass layoffs have brought

employee morale to an all-time low, while employee hos-
tility is at an all-time high. Learning how to laugh while
the sky is falling is a way to maintain one's sanity.

"Laughter is a remedy to reduce tension and motivate
workers," behaviorists tell us. "Humor is an acquired
coping skill and communication tool that gets better with
practice."

Yes, indeed.

Profanity in the Executive Suite

A Colorado management consultant believes in the benefits of "creative swearing."

"Profanity fosters bonding," she said, adding that profanity must be selective—aimed only at the project or
situation, never at people. And, she cautions, swear just
enough for impact. Too many epithets may lead to a
reputation as foul-mouthed.

As for those of us to whom profanity is the equality
of rudeness?

"That's a holier-than-thou attitude that could hurt
teamwork."

. . . And that's just one person's opinion! The bottom
line is that profanity never enhances one's appearance.

How NOT to Handle Complaints

An executive we know is unhappy about the way business
treats the consumer. "If this is a service economy," he
asks, "where's the service?" "Bad enough that we spend
more time standing in lines waiting to buy something
than deciding what it is we want to purchase. But what
I'm talking about is getting satisfaction when something
goes wrong!

"How many times has an employee said to you, 'I'm
so sorry you were inconvenienced. Let me take care of
that for you'?"

"Never, that's how many times," he snorted. "What
you get is excuses. 'I wasn't here, then.' Or, 'It's not my
department,' or 'The person who handles that is on vacation.'

"That is not help. That's a thud. I find that most
people who say they're trying to help me are just trying
to get me to stop talking about what's wrong so they can
tell me why it's not their problem.

"Help is, 'Let me see what I can do for you. Give me your name, and I will get in touch with you one way or the other!'

"Yes," he sighed, "I hear a lot about young people taking responsibility. They're all willing to take responsibility for sales! Sales are no problem. But is there anybody out there who's willing to take responsibility for getting us a little service?"

EXECUTIVE OBLIGATIONS

As every executive worth the position knows, good manners constitute a necessary complement to good business.

In these chapters we have outlined behavior appropriate for the ever-widening gamut of situations, many of them new and possibly unusual, but encountered, nevertheless, by the executive in today's chaotic world.

At all times, *courteous respect* should be the guiding tenet. Courteous respect is not reserved for commercial use only. It is what all of us owe to one another, and what we all deserve, all the time, every day.

What are we to think of the elegantly attired executive who smiles, shakes hands, and bids an important client good-bye, then turns and screams at a doorman, "Where is the moron who parked my car?" Or the executive who insists that her meetings begin one minute before the hour but is consistently late in relieving her teen-age baby-sitter, is always short of cash and pays by check, and forgets to include the overtime? Or the executive who . . . It's possible to compile a catalog of rudeness containing additional illustrations of bullying behavior, but we don't doubt that every reader will be able to supply a matching number of infuriating personal examples.

We are not permitted to treat *some* people badly. Executives do not prove that they are executives by behaving courteously to one another and some other way to those who're not on the team, in the club, part of the network. Exemplary behavior is expected all the time.

When others are rude, incompetent, into power games, it's difficult to avoid trying to match their bad behavior. Practice taking the fraction of a second pause that will end the ripple of rudeness before it spreads. Instead, replace the rudeness with courteous behavior.

Etiquette has never been a nostrum for morality. Knowing how to handle your fork correctly will hardly make you a better person. And yet, if we learn to handle the turmoil of each day with ease; if we remember to treat the people we encounter as courteously as we wish to be treated; if we are fair in showing appreciation to everyone who deserves recognition—won't we at least improve the quality of life around us?

That would be no small success.

INDEX

ABOUT
THE
AUTHORS

Linda Phillips is also co-director of The Executive Etiquette Company, and received her etiquette instruction in London. During her tenure as an administrator of a well-known school of aesthetics, she engineered its national accreditation. She has served as the director of training and education for a leading pharmaceutical company specializing in personal-care products. A former schoolteacher and educational specialist with the Massachusetts Department of Education, Mrs. Phillips has authored numerous articles for professional journals.

She earned her undergraduate degree in psychology and has a master's degree in education.

Wayne Phillips is a college professor and scholar who has researched the history of etiquette. Formally trained in England, Dr. Phillips has conducted etiquette seminars and workshops for thousands of managers in the United States, Europe, and South America. Along with owning an educational-computer consulting firm, he is co-director of The Executive Etiquette Company, which is based in Taunton, Massachusetts.

He holds a master's degree from the University of Connecticut and a doctorate degree from Boston University. He is a member of the faculty at Bridgewater State College in Massachusetts.

Over the years, the Phillipses have built and developed their main business of etiquette training by traveling to the corporate site. During this training, they actually lay out the most formal of place settings so that dining instruction can emphasize practice and application. Upon completion of the training, participants often comment that they can now carry away a life skill. The Phillipses also share with clients their expertise in telephone technique, written communication skills, corporate and professional appearance, and a variety of other topics especially geared to enhance the business professional in social savvy.

BOOK MARK

The text of this book was composed in
the typeface Janson with
display in Futura
by Crane Typesetting Service, Inc.,
West Barnstable, Massachusetts

This book was printed
by Arcata Graphics,
Fairfield, Pennsylvania

BOOK DESIGN BY
ROBERT BULL DESIGN